THE ULTIMATE
HISTORY
QUIZ BOOK

THE ULTIMATE HISTORY QUIZ BOOK

Brian Williams

Bath · New York · Singapore · Hong Kong · Cologne · Delhi
Melbourne · Amsterdam · Johannesburg · Auckland · Shenzhen

This edition published by Parragon in 2010

Parragon
Queen Street House
4 Queen Street
Bath BA1 1HE, UK

Copyright © Parragon Books Ltd 2009

Designed & produced by Design Principals, Warminster

Compiled by Brian Williams

ISBN: 978-1-4454-0546-9

Printed in Malaysia

CONTENTS

PEOPLE & PLACES
QUESTIONS 1-28

WORLD HISTORY 1
QUESTIONS 29-48

POLITICS & POWER
QUESTIONS 49-68

WARS & WARFARE
QUESTIONS 69-96

MODERN TIMES
QUESTIONS 97-120

ADVENTURE & EXPLORATION
QUESTIONS 121-144

WORLD HISTORY 2
QUESTIONS 145-164

CULTURE & SOCIETY
QUESTIONS 165-184

SCIENCE & LIFE
QUESTIONS 185-200

PEOPLE & PLACES
WHO WAS...?

1

The first American to orbit the earth

2

The Apache chief who died in 1909

3

The author of the *Decline and Fall of the Roman Empire*

4

The American dancer killed by her scarf in 1927

5

Norma Jean Baker, in her Hollywood persona

6

Agrippina's matricidal son

7

The governor of Judea from AD 26

8

The son of King David, also king of Israel

9

The humorist who wrote *Tom Sawyer*

10

The best-known of Roman orators

11

The navigator hired by the Mayflower pilgrims in 1620

12

The first woman in space, 1963

PEOPLE & PLACES
WHERE?

1

Where did Benito Juarez lead a revolution?

2

Where did the Olmecs live?

3

In which country was scientist Marie Curie born?

4

Where were the first divided highways (1909)?

5

Where was King Zog deposed in 1946?

6

Where was Peter the Great emperor?

7

Where did the Romans build Hadrian's Wall?

8

Where is the Arc de Triomphe?

9

Where did Vasco Da Gama arrive in 1498?

10

Where did Kublai Khan found the Yuan dynasty?

11

Where did Michelangelo paint a ceiling 1508-12?

12

Where was Gustavus Adolphus king in the 1600s?

PEOPLE & PLACES
DISTINGUISHED WOMEN

1

Where was Nefertiti queen?

2

Which US President did Edith Bolling Galt marry in 1915?

3

At what did Wilma Rudolph excel?

4

In which science was Caroline Herschel distinguished?

5

What nationality was actress Sarah Bernhardt?

6

Who was the third wife of England's King Henry VIII?

7

Under what name was Agnes Gonxha Bojaxhiu famous?

8

Martha Jane Burke became a Western legend as... ?

9

Who was empress of Russia 1762 to 1796?

10

In what profession was Elizabeth Blackwell a pioneer?

11

Whom did Anne Hathaway marry in 1582?

12

What did Mary Baker Eddy start in 1879?

....

1

Whose American dictionary was first published in 1828?

....

2

What went down in the Atlantic, April 15, 1912?

....

3

What was adopted on July 4, 1776?

....

4

On what date did Britain enter World War II?

....

5

Which American settlement was founded in 1607?

....

6

What year did the Federal government move to Washington?

....

7

Whose tomb did Howard Carter find in 1922?

....

8

What is special about 22 March in the Roman Catholic Church calendar?

....

9

Whose term of office ends at 12 noon on January 20?

....

10

Which country gained independence August 15, 1947?

....

11

What year was the Louisiana Purchase?

....

12

Which war ended in 1763, with the Treaty of Paris?

....

1

Who composed the musical tribute to "Sir Duke," 1977?

2

Where was Crispus Attucks killed in 1770?

3

On what ship did slaves mutiny in 1837?

4

Who led a slave revolt in Virginia in 1831?

5

Who published *The Liberator* (1831-65)?

6

Which newspaper did Frederick Douglass launch in 1847?

7

In Dred Scott v. Sandford, who was Scott?

8

Along what did Harriet Tubman lead escaping slaves?

9

In what field did George Washington Carver research?

10

Who became principal of Tuskegee College, 1881?

11

Who wrote *The Souls of Black Folk* (1903)?

12

Who in the 1920s urged blacks to move to Africa?

PEOPLE & PLACES
MEMORABLE WORDS

1

"You ain't heard nothing yet, folks" was said by... ?

2

Who did Henry Lee call "First in war, first in peace... "

3

Who said "we must consult Brother Jonathan"?

4

Who said "please sir, I want some more"?

5

Which German statesman said "politics is no exact science"?

6

Which Ancient Greek said "Eureka!"?

7

For what did an 1888 ad claim, "You press the button and we'll do the rest"?

8

Who queried "how many divisions" the pope had (1935)?

9

Which president had a notice saying "the buck stops here"?

10

Who said, "Dr Livingstone, I presume?"

11

Who called the Owl "you elegant fowl"?

12

Who said, "give us the tools and we will finish the job"?

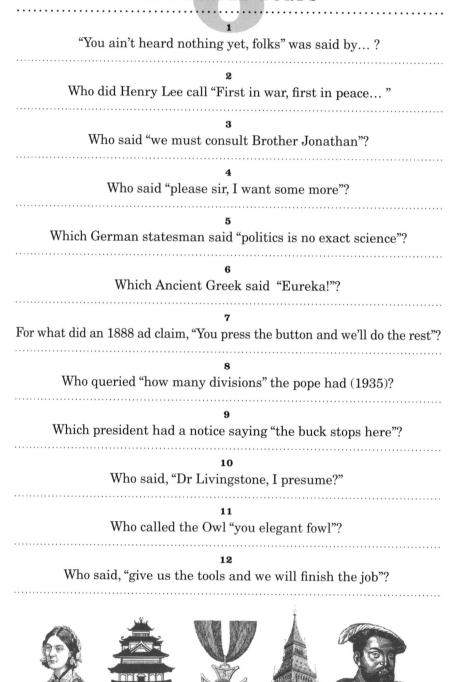

1

Siam is the old name for... ?

2

Dahomey is the old name for... ?

3

The Gold Coast is a former name for which African state?

4

What was Zimbabwe called when a British colony?

5

What is British Honduras known as today?

6

Cathay is an old name for... ?

7

New Amsterdam is now known as... ?

8

What was Van Diemen's Land later renamed?

9

The Indian city of Bombay is now known as... ?

10

What was Lesotho called before 1966?

11

What was St Petersburg known as in the Soviet era?

12

By what name is South West Africa known today?

PEOPLE & PLACES
AMERICAN MISCELLANY

1

What honor did Gwendolyn Brooks win in 1950?

2

Which bridge (1883) did John Roebling design?

3

Who succeeded John Carver as Plymouth Colony governor?

4

Who was known to Boy Scouts as "Uncle Dan"?

5

Of whom was Black Kettle a famous leader?

6

Which singer/actor was born in Tacoma 1903, died 1977?

7

Who was first African American head of the Joint Chiefs of Staff?

8

Who wrote *Walden* (1854)?

9

In what was Jackie Robinson a star?

10

Where was Orval E. Faubus governor in 1957?

11

What party did Huey Newton and Bobby Seale found?

12

What office did Ross Perot seek in 1992 and 1996?

PEOPLE & PLACES
BIRTHS AND DEATHS

. . . .

1

Who was killed at Ford's Theatre in 1865?

. . . .

2

In which English palace near Oxford was Winston Churchill born?

. . . .

3

What did Pierre de Coubertin, born in 1863, revive?

. . . .

4

Who was the first director of the FBI, born in 1895?

. . . .

5

Which American detective was born in Scotland, 1819?

. . . .

6

Who wrote *The Scarlet Pimpernel,* and was born 1865?

. . . .

7

Who was the author of *Dracula*, died 1912?

. . . .

8

Who was the American childcare guru, born 1903?

. . . .

9

Who wrote *The Godfather,* born New York 1920?

. . . .

10

Who was the first to the South Pole, born Norway 1872?

. . . .

11

Who wrote *The Catcher in the Rye*, and died in 2010?

. . . .

12

Who wrote *Jane Eyre* and died during pregnancy in 1855?

. . . .

1

Whom did Robert Ford shoot dead in 1882?

2

For what crimes was Captain Kidd hanged in 1701?

3

FBI agent (died 1957), he pursued Al Capone. Who was he?

4

Where were Davy Crockett and Jim Bowie killed in 1836?

5

How did Casey Jones become a folk hero?

6

America's most famous historical turncoat, lived 1741-1801?

7

How did Joan of Arc die in 1431?

8

Which gangster duo were shot dead in 1934?

9

How did Gestapo boss Heinrich Himmler die, May 23, 1945?

10

What did William Tell shoot off his son's head?

11

In the Old English story, whom did Beowulf slay?

12

Who commanded the ship *Bonhomme Richard* in 1779?

PEOPLE & PLACES
WHO SAID IT?

. . . .

1

Who said (more than once) "We must consult Brother Jonathan"?

. . . .

2

Who said in 1850 "I shall die an American"?

. . . .

3

Which lawyer (1782-1852) said "There's always room at the top"?

. . . .

4

What did Voltaire say God was always on the side of?

. . . .

5

Which American writer's last words (1910) began "turn up the lights..."?

. . . .

6

Which American poet (1830-86) wrote "How dreary to be somebody"?

. . . .

7

Which president coined the phrase "rugged individualism" in 1928?

. . . .

8

Who reputedly said "There's a sucker born every minute"?

. . . .

9

Which American statesman said "remember that time is money"?

. . . .

10

Which president said "let us never fear to negotiate"?

. . . .

11

Who urged "workers of the world, unite"?

. . . .

12

Who said "every soldier carries a marshal's baton"?

. . . .

PEOPLE & PLACES
POTPOURRI

1

Where was George VI replaced by a president in 1949?

2

Who was Ghana's first president (1960)?

3

Where was the Bastille attacked in 1789?

4

What kind of craft did in John Fitch invent in 1787?

5

What did Clyde Tombaugh spot in 1930?

6

How did Umberto Nobile travel to the Pole in 1926?

7

Who went to Harpers Ferry in 1859?

8

How did Mary Queen of Scots die?

9

Which country had the first female prime minister?

10

Who was Kit Carson?

11

Which winter sports event was first held at St Moritz in 1884?

12

What are Flathead, Blackfoot, and Hopi?

PEOPLE & PLACES
GENERAL KNOWLEDGE

1

What sports event took place in Mexico in 1970?

2

Which US city had the first paid fire dept. (1679)?

3

Where did the Great Trek take place in 1836?

4

Which treaty ended the Napoleonic Wars?

5

Where was a "Tea Party" held in 1773?

6

Who lived at Monticello?

7

In which war was the Battle of Mobile Bay?

8

Where were Omaha and Sword?

9

Which general captured Pensacola in 1814?

10

Where did the Capetian kings reign?

11

What was Susanna Salter's distinction, 1887?

12

Who was born in Khomein, Iran, about 1900?

PEOPLE & PLACES
WHO WERE THEY?

14

1

Who founded the corporation that built the DC-3 airplane?

2

Who served as LBJ's vice president?

3

Recited "Mary had a little lamb" in 1877?

4

Born 1874, three times prime minister of Canada?

5

Wrote *The Last of the Mohicans* (1826)?

6

First African-American mayor of Los Angeles?

7

Founder of the American Library Association (1876)?

8

Country singer who died in 1953, at the age of 29?

9

Composer of "Appalachian Spring" (1940)?

10

Brazilian, in born 1940, the "king of soccer"?

11

American golfer, born Atlanta, Ga., 1902. Who was he?

12

Ruler of Iran until 1979?

1

In which state is Whitfield House, dating from 1629?

2

Where is there a reconstruction of Fort King George?

3

In which state is Old Narrangansett Church?

4

In which city was Harvard founded in 1836?

5

Where were Forts Atkinson and Robinson built?

6

In which state is Historic Fort Wayne?

7

Where is the National Cowboy Hall of Fame?

8

In which state was the co-ed Oberlin College founded?

9

In which state is Independence Rock?

10

In which state was Fort Ross built, by Russians?

11

Which Texan city was briefly capital of Missouri?

12

In which state can you see Trenton Old Barracks?

21

PEOPLE & PLACES
BUILDINGS IN HISTORY

1

Whose official residence is 10 Downing Street, London?

2

Where was the Space Needle built in 1962?

3

Baroque architecture is typical of which two centuries?

4

Which city has the Folger Shakespeare Library?

5

In which century was the Gothic revival in architecture?

6

In which city is the Gothic-style St Patrick's Cathedral?

7

Who designed The Willits House, 1902?

8

In which royal British castle did fire break out, 20 Nov. 1992?

9

Who built Fort Casimir in 1631?

10

Where was the Reliance Building erected, 1894?

11

In which state was Fort Bridger built in 1843?

12

What year was the Empire State Building completed?

PEOPLE & PLACES
FAMOUS QUOTES

1

Who described England as a nation of shopkeepers?

2

Who said Russia was "a riddle wrapped in a mystery"?

3

Which politician said he was "on the side of the angels"?

4

When was the slogan "Remember the Maine" used?

5

Who asked, " What are we to do with this bauble?"

6

Voters in 1952 wore badges saying "I like Ike." Who was Ike?

7

Which president declared he was a Berliner in 1963?

8

Which Soviet leader said in 1956 "We will bury you"?

9

Where did Martin Luther King make his "I have a dream" speech?

10

Who said (in 1940) "the US must be the arsenal of democracy"?

11

Who in 1942 told the Philippines "I shall return"?

12

Which Chinese leader called the United States "a paper tiger"?

PEOPLE & PLACES
NATIVE AMERICAN HISTORY

· ·

1

In which Indian war of 1832 did Lincoln take part?

2

Which was the largest city in pre-Columbian America?

3

Which Native Americans built hogans?

4

What is buckskin?

5

What was "snow snake"?

6

What did Incas use quipus for?

7

What are Folsom points?

8

What was a parfleche?

9

What happened at a potlatch?

10

What does "pueblo" mean?

11

Who or what was a sachem?

12

Who was killed resisting arrest at Standing Rock, 1890?

PEOPLE & PLACES
BADDIES AND GOODIES

1

What was Lizzie Borden's alleged murder weapon?

2

Who was admired as the "great soul"?

3

Which gangster was jailed for not paying taxes?

4

Of which country is Garibaldi a national hero?

5

Which Scottish hero became known as Braveheart?

6

Who were said to have demonic "familiars"?

7

What was Blackbeard the pirate's real name?

8

Which American author wrote about Nick and Nora Charles (1934)?

9

In which country did El Cid become a national hero?

10

Which American sailor won the Battle of Lake Erie, 1813?

11

Who was the most-decorated American soldier of World War II?

12

Whose mystic powers fascinated Czarina Alexandra?

1

Who wrote *The Rights of Man*, 1792?

2

Which king granted Carolina to colonists in 1663?

3

Whom did Thelma Catherine Ryan marry in 1940?

4

Who said "I have not yet begun to fight"?

5

In which performing art was Agnes de Mille prominent?

6

Which writer created the character of Perry Mason?

7

Who started their circus at Bonaboo in 1884?

8

Who said in 1912 "Liberty is its own reward"?

9

Born Frances Gumm in 1922, who was she?

10

Whose wife was Martha Dandridge Custis?

11

Who sang at the Lincoln Memorial in 1939?

12

Who ran for president 5 times, and never was?

1

Italian violinist virtuoso (1782-1840)?

2

American writer known for her wit (1893-1967)?

3

World War II general nicknamed "Old Blood and Guts"?

4

Greek philosopher who taught at the Academy?

5

Spanish conqueror of Peru?

6

Native American who married John Rolfe in 1616?

7

American who invented the train sleeping car, 1863?

8

Rock 'n' roll legend who died in 1977?

9

President of Argentina from 1895 to 1974?

10

American who set up annual prizes for journalism?

11

Spanish painter born aged 81, died 1973?

12

Greek statesman who led Athens in the 400s BC?

PEOPLE & PLACES
POTPOURRI

1

Which president was born at West Branch, Iowa?

2

Who beat Jesse Jackson for presidential nomination in 1998?

3

Who partnered Oliver Hardy on-screen?

4

Who was the youngest-ever First Lady?

5

Who became governor of Arkansas in 1983?

6

Who in 1830 got a job as a store clerk at New Salem, Illinois?

7

Where is Paul Revere's House?

8

Which explorer landed on Vancouver Island in 1778?

9

Which Alaskan city was originally "Ship Creek"?

10

What came from London to Lake Havasu City in 1971?

11

Of which Native Americans was Black Kettle a leader?

12

Which university did James Meredith attend?

1

What did Squanto teach the colonists?

2

What did Peter Minuit buy?

3

By what name was Metacomet known to the colonists?

4

What were "redemptioners"?

5

Who arrived at Jamestown in 1619?

6

What was the House of Burgesses?

7

What was a trundle bed?

8

Where were the first ironworks in colonial America?

9

Which cities were linked by the Boston Post Road?

10

Which city had America's first newspaper?

11

17 women, 3 men, executed at Salem, 1692—for what?

12

What did the colonial "blue laws" regulate?

PEOPLE & PLACES
SOME MORE FAMOUS AMERICANS

1

Directed the movie *It's a Wonderful Life* and others?

2

First black world heavyweight boxing champion, 1908?

3

US general born Little Rock, Arkansas, 1880?

4

America's fifth president, born in 1758?

5

Which movie star gave birth to a daughter called Apple in 2004?

6

Author of *The Rise and Fall of the Third Reich* (1960)?

7

Victor over the Seminoles at Okeechobee Swamp, in 1837?

8

Choreographer and modern dance pioneer, born Pittsburgh 1904?

9

Famous for "marching to the sea" in 1864?

10

African-American baseball star born Cairo, Georgia 1919

11

Secretary of State under President Truman 1949 to 1953?

12

Star of TV's Texaco Star Theater 1948-56?

PEOPLE & PLACES
COUPLES

1

Who was the wife of Czar Nicholas II?

2

Who was Josephine's famous husband?

3

Can you name Queen Victoria's husband?

4

Who lured Mark Antony up the Nile?

5

In Shakespeare's play, with whom did Juliet fall in love?

6

Whose First Lady was Mamie Geneva Doud?

7

What fruit did Nell Gwyn supposedly offer King Charles II of England?

8

Who fell for Mrs Simpson?

9

Who was the famous TV partner of Desi Arnaz?

10

Which poet did Elizabeth Barrett fall for?

11

Whom did Jacqueline Lee Bouvier marry in 1953?

12

Who was Ginger Rogers' most famous dance partner?

1

Which country singer was born 1932 at Kingsland, Arkansas?

2

Where did William B. Travis die in 1836?

3

Which Texan city served as Missouri's capital 1863 to 1865?

4

In which sport did Bill Tilden star in the 1920s?

5

Where did John T. Scopes teach school in 1925?

6

Which city enjoyed the first TV broadcasts, 1936?

7

What was Virginia Dare's claim to fame?

8

Which library started in 1800 with a $5000 grant?

9

In which city was the Olds Motor Works founded 1899?

10

Which world title did Phil Hill win in 1961?

11

What was General Grant's first name?

12

Which heiress got mixed up with the Symbionese Liberation Army?

PEOPLE & PLACES
MORE PEOPLE AND PLACES

1

In which state is Bent's Old Fort?

2

Who was Henry Cowell (1897-1965)?

3

What are vaqueros?

4

Which is the only US territory visited by Columbus?

5

Which famous building burned down in 1814?

6

In which state was the Battle of Mount Pleasant, 1774?

7

Who wrote *Charlotte's Web* (1952)?

8

In which mountain range is the Donner Pass?

9

What tragedy struck in the Donner Pass, 1846-47?

10

What institutions did Alphonse Desjardins pioneer (1900)?

11

Which Canadian city has a citadel on Cape Diamond?

12

What did George Bancroft found in 1845?

1

Which city was the "Queen City of the West"?

2

In which city was America's first public school?

3

In which city is Beehive House, dating from 1855?

4

Which colonial city had America's first street lights?

5

In which city is the restored port of Strawbery Banke?

6

Which city was founded by Sieur de Bienville, in 1718?

7

In which city was King's College founded in 1754?

8

What led to the founding of Nome in Alaska in 1899?

9

In which Canadian city did the Lachine Canal open in 1825?

10

Which is further north, Boston or New York?

11

Which city did Henry M. Flagler's railroad reach in 1896?

12

What was an early nickname for Fort Worth, Texas?

WORLD HISTORY 1
ANCIENT (1)

1

What were iguanodon and diplodocus?

2

How was Piltdown Man not what he seemed?

3

Who or what were Cro-Magnon?

4

Which early humans had much bigger noses than ours?

5

What does "Neolithic" mean?

6

How did Britain change around 6500 BC?

7

Which elephant-like mammals roamed Ice Age Europe?

8

What was the aurochs?

9

What did early farmers do with an "ard"?

10

What kind of stone was best for tool-making?

11

Where was "Otzi the Iceman" found in 1991?

12

Which ancient stone circle stands on England's Salisbury Plain?

WORLD HISTORY 1
ANCIENT (2)

1

Where was the Temple of Amun?

2

Whose capital was Knossos?

3

Where is Abu Simbel?

4

What was the Exodus?

5

What were the Phoenicians good at?

6

Where was Nebuchadnezzar I king?

7

Where did the Yellow Emperor reign?

8

Why did the Maya think 3372 a big number?

9

Which kingdom did Menes unite under his rule?

10

Where did Hammurabi make the laws?

11

On which river did Mohenjo-Daro flourish?

12

Where was the empire of Kush?

WORLD HISTORY 1
WORLD WAR I

1

Who were shot by Gavrilo Princip?

2

What relation was George V to Kaiser Wilhelm?

3

In which European country was the battlefield of Ypres?

4

What year was the "Christmas Truce"?

5

Why did officers at the Front stop wearing swords?

6

What war service did Ernest Hemingway undertake?

7

Who was Mata Hari?

8

Who changed their name to Windsor?

9

Which ocean liner was sunk by a German submarine in May 1915?

10

Who had a Fourteen-Point peace plan in 1918?

11

What date did World War I end in Europe?

12

For which warring nation was Erich Ludendorff a general?

1

Who were Jefferson's two vice presidents?

2

What do vice presidents Calhoun and Agnew have in common?

3

To whom was Dan Quayle vice president 1989-93?

4

Which of these became president: Coolidge, Ford, Gore?

5

Where were vice presidents sworn in until 1933?

6

Who was president for eight hours in 1985?

7

Who succeeded a president who had resigned?

8

Youngest vice president to succeed a dead president?

9

Vice president who succeeded F.D. Roosevelt?

10

Who was LBJ's number two?

11

Who was Bill Clinton's vice president?

12

Who was Ike's vice president (and later president)?

WORLD HISTORY 1
WHICH CENTURY WAS...?

1

The Austrian War of Succession

2

Napoleon born

3

The Mexican-American War

4

The Battle of Agincourt

5

The Battle of Hastings

6

Siege of Constantinople

7

The Spanish Armada

8

The Thirty Years' War

9

The Seven Years' War

10

The Battle of Jutland

11

The Battle of Rorke's Drift

12

The Battle of Bull Run

1

Which Balkans ruler stuck people on stakes?

2

Where was the 1637 Pequot Massacre?

3

Where was the St Bartholomew's Day Massacre?

4

How did Inca ruler Tupac Ameru die in 1572?

5

What killed 10,000 in Lisbon, 1755?

6

Where was Bernard de Launay killed in 1789?

7

What killed 132,000 people in Tokyo, in 1923?

8

Hulegu's army razed Baghdad in 1258. Who were they?

9

During which war was the Massacre at Babi Yar?

10

Which Spanish city's bombing was immortalized by the artist Picasso?

11

Where was Michael Servetus burned at the stake in 1553?

12

What was the Massacre of Wounded Knee?

WORLD HISTORY 1
BRITISH ROYAL TRIVIA

1

Who spent the war years as governor of the Bahamas?

2

Which British royal prince was born 21 June 1982?

3

Who were married on 20 November 1947?

4

Which queen had an Australian state named after her?

5

Whose marriage took place on 29 July 1981?

6

Who died in a car crash, 31 August 1997?

7

Who was Britain's king at the time of the American War of Independence?

8

Which king came from Scotland to succeed Elizabeth I in 1603?

9

Who was Britain's king during World War I?

10

Which English king had six wives?

11

Which princess did Anthony Armstrong-Jones marry?

12

Which English king's first language was German?

FAMOUS PARENTS & CHILDREN

1

Who was the father of King Henry V of England?

2

Who was husband to Rosalynn and father to Amy?

3

Who was the mother of Mary Queen of Scots?

4

Whose baby son was kidnapped and murdered in March 1932?

5

Who is the second child of Queen Elizabeth II?

6

Beatrice and Eugenie are whose daughters?

7

Whose parents were Rose and Joseph P.?

8

Who was Thomas and Nancy's son, born 12 February 1809?

9

Which president's parents were ambassador Joe and wife Rose?

10

Who were the parents of Louis XIV of France?

11

Who was the famous son of Pepin, King of the Franks?

12

Who was Martha Randolph's famous father?

WORLD HISTORY 1
MIDDLE AGES

1

Whose court is described in the *Thousand And One Nights*?

2

What does "Charlemagne" mean?

3

Where did Charlemagne found a school?

4

Where did Charles Martel defeat the Moors in 732?

5

How did Frederick Barbarossa get his name?

6

Which city did Saracens capture in 1187?

7

What was Timur Lenk's other name?

8

How did this Mongol warrior get his name?

9

Which religious teacher was born at Assisi in 1182?

10

Where was Angkor Wat built in the 1100s?

11

What was a moat?

12

Who lived and worked in monasteries?

WORLD HISTORY 1
RENAISSANCE EUROPE

1

Who was known as Il Moro?

2

What did Erasmus hope to reform?

3

Where did Calvin move to from France?

4

Which Spanish kingdom did Ferdinand rule from 1479?

5

Which artist wrote in "mirror writing"?

6

Who was known as Il Magnifico?

7

Who met at the Council of Trent?

8

Who fell in love with a Russian slave, Roxalana?

9

What did he do for her?

10

In which European country did artists Michelangelo and Raphael work?

11

Which French king said "Paris is worth a mass"?

12

Why did he say it?

WORLD HISTORY 1
GREEKS AND GREEK MYTHS

1

Who dined on ambrosia?

2

What was a lyre?

3

What were hoplites?

4

Who flung thunderbolts?

5

How many Muses were there?

6

Which bull-headed monster devoured human victims?

7

And on which island did it live (according to legend)?

8

Which were the two strongest Greek cities?

9

Whom did the Greeks call "barbarians"?

10

Who was the Greek goddess of wisdom and war?

11

What were oracles?

12

Which is the most famous Greek temple?

1

Against whom did Romans revolt in 510?

2

What was lorica segmentata?

3

What did Roman soldiers use for toilet paper?

4

Where did Aulus Plautius invade?

5

What was a ballista?

6

How did the Roman Army use Numidians?

7

What did a slinger sling?

8

How many men made up a cohort: 20, 500, 5000?

9

What was a signum?

10

What did a centurion carry, to show rank?

11

What was a cataphract?

12

What shape was the standard legionary shield?

WORLD HISTORY 1
1600s-1700s

1

Who said "I think, therefore I am"?

2

Which French general fought with Washington at Valley Forge?

3

In which continent was the 1757 battle of Plassey?

4

What year was the British surrender at Yorktown?

5

Which Chinese dynasty ended in 1644?

6

Whose soldiers were known as "Ironsides"?

7

What title was he given in 1653?

8

What was Catherine the Great's first language?

9

How long did her husband Peter last as czar of Russia?

10

What nationality was Marie Antoinette?

11

Who was her husband?

12

How did she die?

WORLD HISTORY 1
ANCIENT CIVILIZATIONS

. . . .

1

In what modern country are the ruins of Ur?

. . . .

2

Which people lived at Ur?

. . . .

3

What was cuneiform?

. . . .

4

Who led his people to Canaan?

. . . .

5

Where did his journey begin?

. . . .

6

Whose chief cities were Assur and Nineveh?

. . . .

7

Where was the Ishtar Gate?

. . . .

8

Which king built the Hanging Gardens?

. . . .

9

Why are step pyramids so called?

. . . .

10

Where was Thebes a capital city?

. . . .

11

Whose wife was Nefertiti?

. . . .

12

Where did the Jomon people live?

. . . .

WORLD HISTORY 1
ANCIENT TIMES

....

1

Where was the emperor called the Son of Heaven?

....

2

Where was the Nok culture?

....

3

Where did Socrates teach?

....

4

Which philosopher taught Alexander the Great?

....

5

Which empire did Tigranes (Dikran) found in 95 BC?

....

6

And who conquered it soon after?

....

7

With which two Romans did Cleopatra have liaisons?

....

8

Which people left frozen tombs in the Altai Mountains?

....

9

What part of Europe did Thracians inhabit?

....

10

Whose language survives in Welsh and Gaelic?

....

11

Who was Bleda's famous brother?

....

12

And what happened to Bleda?

....

1

Whose daughter was Indira Gandhi?

2

Born Braunau, Austria 1889; who was he?

3

Which world leader went into a coma in January 2006?

4

First leader of independent Pakistan (1947)?

5

In which part of Britain did the Stuart dynasty originate?

6

Where was De Gaulle president?

7

What number president is Barrack Obama?

8

Which emperor edited Russia's first newspaper?

9

Which Byzantine emperor was married to Theodora?

10

Who officially opened the Panama Canal?

11

Which president liked to be known as the Gipper?

12

Which president brought in Prohibition?

WORLD HISTORY 1
1600-1620

1

Where was Jamestown?

2

Who was England's "virgin Queen"?

3

Where did the "false Dmitri" lead a rising?

4

Who was the Native American Indian Princess who married John Rolfe?

5

In which art form did Monteverdi make his name?

6

What building was England's 1605 "gunpowder plot" attempting to blow up?

7

Henri IV was assassinated in 1610; where was he king?

8

Which Bay in Canada was discovered in 1610?

9

In which English colony did the first African slaves arrive, 1619?

10

Which scientist appeared before the Inquisition in 1616?

11

What ship landed in New England in 1620?

12

Where was Richelieu in charge of foreign policy?

1

In May 1707, which three countries united to form the kingdom of Great Britain?

2

Wrote *The Prince*, born May 3, 1469: who was this Italian?

3

Who killed himself with his mistress in the ruins of Berlin, May 1945?

4

Which German airship came down in flames on May 6, 1937?

5

Then the world's tallest building, completed 1931?

6

What was the U-2, shot down over Red territory?

7

Born May 1819, who wrote "The Battle Hymn of the Republic"?

8

May 21, 1927, who completed a solo Atlantic flight?

9

Which famous American bridge opened to traffic, 24 May 1883?

10

What year did the first regular US airmail service begin?

11

Which president was born in Lamar, Mo., May 8, 1884

12

The first reigning British monarch to visit Canada, in May 1939?

1

Can you name India's beautiful imperial tomb at Agra?

2

Of which organization did M.K. Gandhi become leader in 1920?

3

Who was assassinated on 30 January 1948?

4

With which country did India go to war in 1962?

5

Which region was disputed between India and Pakistan?

6

Which Portuguese colony did India reclaim in 1961?

7

Which part of Pakistan did Indian troops enter in 1971?

8

Which Indian leader was assassinated in 1991?

9

Who succeeded Indira Gandhi in October 1984?

10

Who was overthrown by the Pakistan Army in 1977?

11

Which woman became Pakistan premier in 1988?

12

Father and daughter, both prominent in Pakistan's politics. Name?

1

In which war was the song *Over There* a hit?

2

In which decade was the Scopes trial?

3

Who was Billy Sunday?

4

Who began the New Deal in 1933?

5

What were "Hoovervilles"?

6

What was the Dust Bowl?

7

Who led the United States into World War II?

8

In which state was Little Rock, scene of the "crisis" in 1957?

9

What did Eisenhower authorize there in 1957?

10

Which two states joined the Union in 1959?

11

Who was the first American in space, in 1961?

12

Where did the 1963 Freedom March take place?

POLITICS & POWER
RULING DYNASTIES

1

In which country did the House of Valois reign?

2

Where did the Hohenzollerns hold power?

3

Where did the Habsburgs rule?

4

Romanovs ruled which country?

5

Name two countries ruled by Bourbons.

6

The Meiji was a period of rule in which country?

7

Who was India's leader Nehru's famous daughter?

8

Where did Edo rulers hold sway?

9

Long-serving US senator, and Kennedy clan leader, died 2009?

10

In which medieval country were Lancaster and York rivals for a crown?

11

What year did the Romanov dynasty lose power?

12

Where was the Ming dynasty the ruling power?

POLITICS & POWER
THE NAME'S THE SAME

1

Capote the writer, and the 33rd US president

2

Auto tycoon and US president

3

US president, and a legendary king with a round table

4

Female star of *Some Like It Hot*, and a president

5

First pope and Russian czar

6

One-time Democrat hopeful, playwright, silent movie cowboy

7

Vacuum cleaner and US president

8

Indian prime minister and advocate of non-violence

9

American frontier soldier (1700s) and Fred's dancing partner

10

Geographic pole and a UK prime minister

11

Controversial US senator and female novelist who wrote *The Group*

12

A US president and UK prime minister

POLITICS & POWER
AMERICAN PRESIDENTS

1

Who wrote a book titled *Where's the Rest of Me*?

2

Who was sworn in as president on a plane?

3

Who was the first president to speak on radio?

4

What were John Kennedy's "firsts" in 1960?

5

Who was the oldest person to be elected president?

6

Which president had no political party?

7

Which president was born in Hope, Arkansas in 1946?

8

Was Abraham Lincoln a Republican or a Democrat?

9

Which president preceded Franklin D. Roosevelt?

10

Eight of the first ten presidents were... what (profession)?

11

Which president was a general in the Civil War?

12

Which president never married?

1

Who was the second president of the United States?

2

What year did Winston Churchill become British prime minister?

3

Who presided during the US "Panic of 1837"?

4

Who followed Mrs Thatcher as British prime minister?

5

Of which country was Georges Pompidou president?

6

Address in London, England, of the British prime minister?

7

Which president succeeded Jimmy Carter?

8

Whose motto was "speak softly and carry a big stick"?

9

Which ex-premier of Pakistan was murdered in 2007?

10

Where was Brian Mulroney prime minister?

11

Bob Hawke led which country?

12

How many fathers and sons have been presidents?

POLITICS & POWER
THE RUSSIAN REVOLUTION

1

What month and year was the Russian Revolution?

2

Who led the Bolsheviks?

3

Who was forced to give up his throne?

4

Who were murdered at Ekaterinburg?

5

How did February become March in 1918?

6

What was St Petersburg renamed in 1914?

7

Who was Alexander Kerensky?

8

What did the treaty of Brest-Litovsk end?

9

Which city was Russia's capital after the revolution?

10

What did the revolutionaries call their army?

11

Who were the Reds and Whites?

12

The title of John Reed's book about the revolution?

POLITICS & POWER
POLITICAL WHO'S WHO?

1

Pierre T., Canadian prime minister

2

Mikhail G., Russian reformer

3

Kofi A., UN Secretary-General

4

Joe B., Democratic vice president

5

Robert M. G., Secretary of Defense

6

Willy B., West German leader

7

Dmitry M., Russian president in 2008

8

Sarah P., ran alongside John McCain

9

Arnold S., Governor of California

10

Nicolas S., elected French president 2007

11

Dan Q., US vice president

12

Boris Y., Russian president

BALLOT BOX

POLITICS & POWER
POLITICAL LOSERS

1

Who lost to Kennedy in 1963?

2

To whom did Kerensky lose out in Russia 1917?

3

Who was narrowly beaten by George W. Bush in 2000?

4

With whom did Lincoln debate seven times in 1858?

5

Who beat John McCain to the White House?

6

Which party lost power in the UK in 1997?

7

Which French queen lost her head on the guillotine?

8

Who resigned as Britain's prime minister in 1940?

9

Who lost to Roosevelt in 1940?

10

To whom did George Bush Sr. lose the 1992 election?

11

Who defeated Adlai Stevenson in 1952 and 1956?

12

Who beat Hubert Humphrey in 1968?

1

Who governed Batavia?

2

Which countries made up French Indochina?

3

Which European state colonized Madagascar?

4

Where did Kublai Khan sit on the imperial throne?

5

From where did the US depose a queen in 1893?

6

Which animal symbolized the British Empire?

7

Which ancient empire was founded by Cyrus the Great?

8

Which empire did Asoka rule?

9

Where did British rule replace French in 1882?

10

Where were the Ashanti defeated in 1896?

11

In which continent was the Empire of Mali?

12

Which African kingdom did Italy grab in 1889?

BALLOT BOX

POLITICS & POWER
POLITICAL FIRSTS

1

Leader of first black slaves' revolt in Haiti, 1791?

2

Britain's first woman prime minister?

3

First president to win the Nobel Peace Prize?

4

First president to give regular press conferences?

5

First president to live in the White House?

6

First and only president to resign?

7

First chancellor of a reunited Germany?

8

First president sworn in by a woman ?

9

First shots in the American Revolution, April 19, 1775. Where?

10

First woman president of the Irish Republic?

11

First woman to be elected to the US Senate?

12

First time American women voted for the president?

POLITICS & POWER
POT LUCK (1)

1

What did the D in Franklin D. Roosevelt stand for?

2

Where did Beatrix become queen in 1980?

3

Where did Victor Emmanuel become king in 1861?

4

Of which country was Leopold I king in 1831?

5

Who was France's "Citizen King" 1813 to 1848?

6

What do the initials IRA stand for?

7

Who became emperor of the French, 1804?

8

Year of the first elections to the European Parliament?

9

Who was the last tsar of Russia?

10

How many of Henry VIII's wives lost their heads?

11

Which country's leader was the Caudillo?

12

Where did Evita (Eva Peron) wow the crowds?

POLITICS & POWER
AROUND THE WORLD

1

How was Lev Davidovitch Bronstein better known?

2

Where was Pierre Trudeau twice prime minister?

3

Which Czech leader was overthrown in 1969?

4

In which country did Nasser nationalize a canal?

5

Who was first Chancellor of West Germany?

6

Russian Czar Ivan IV's nickname was... ?

7

Which country did Mustafa Kemal modernize?

8

First prime minister of independent India?

9

Where did Lech Walesa lead a workers' movement?

10

Which country had two kings named Carol?

11

Albert Bernard Bongo ruled where until 2009?

12

Who were "B and K", in the news in the 1950s?

POLITICS & POWER
FAMOUS WOMEN

1

Which English queen defied the might of Spain in 1588?

2

Who was the "Iron Lady"?

3

What relation was Queen Mary I of England to Elizabeth I?

4

Against whom did the Ancient British queen Boudicca fight?

5

Whose wife was Queen Elizabeth, the Queen Mother?

6

Which First Lady was known as "Lady Bird"?

7

With which Indian city was Mother Teresa associated?

8

Who was the first American woman in space?

9

Which 2 women led a US women's rights convention in 1848?

10

Which English king married Eleanor of Aquitaine?

11

Whom did Eva Braun marry in 1945?

12

Which French queen probably never said "let them eat cake"?

POLITICS & POWER
US POLITICAL FIGURES

1

Name the only president who was also speaker of the House.

2

Who led the newly formed AFL in 1886?

3

Who was chosen to succeed Monroe as president in 1824?

4

And his rival, who set up a breakaway party?

5

Which president arranged the Louisiana Purchase of 1803?

6

Who was America's first African American woman senator?

7

In which city did Harold Washington become mayor in 1983?

8

What year did Bush succeed Reagan as president?

9

Whose vice president was Charles W. Fairbanks?

10

What office did Cordell Hull hold, 1933 to 1944?

11

Which Republicans ran for president and vice president in 1996?

12

What first did Shirley Chisholm achieve?

POLITICS & POWER
FAMOUS IN THEIR DAY

1

Where was Ferdinand Marcos president 1965-86?

2

Who ordered the invasion of Britain in AD 43?

3

Who was the second US president to be assassinated?

4

Where did Sukarno hold power, 1945 to 1966?

5

Where did Golda Meir hold power 1968-74?

6

Who was Japan's emperor during World War II?

7

What post did Harry A. Blackmun hold from 1970 to 1994?

8

Who was probably the heaviest president, at about 300 pounds?

9

Who was England's monarch when Shakespeare was born?

10

Who was Michael Collins?

11

Who was Sir Mackenzie Bowell?

12

Of which country was P.W. Botha leader?

POLITICS & POWER
NATIONAL LEADERS

1

Which British statesman won the Nobel Prize for Literature?

2

Which country did Frederick the Great rule?

3

Where did Benito Juarez lead a revolution?

4

Who took power in Libya in 1969?

5

Who succeeded Lenin as Soviet leader in 1922?

6

Where did Kossuth lead a revolution in 1848?

7

Who became Mexico's president in 1934?

8

Who became leader of Gran Colombia in 1819?

9

Of which country was Julius Nyerere leader?

10

Where was Sir Robert Borden government leader 1911-20?

11

In which country did Bernardo O'Higgins achieve fame?

12

Of which European state was Gustavus I king from 1523?

POLITICS & POWER
DICTATORS AND DESPOTS

1

Where did Papa Doc rule?

2

Where was Ceausescu dictator?

3

Where did Salazar hold power?

4

Where was Pol Pot's reign of terror?

5

Which country did Idi Amin terrorize?

6

Who was known as Il Duce?

7

Who was found hiding in a cellar in 2003?

8

Where did Kim Il Sung rule?

9

Whose purges in the 1930s killed millions?

10

Where did Enver Hoxha rule?

11

Which African dictator proclaimed himself Emperor?

12

Where did Robert Mugabe rule?

BALLOT BOX

POLITICS & POWER
PLACES OF POWER

1

What year did the White House get that name officially?

2

Name the Frenchman who planned Washington DC (1790s).

3

Who lives in the Elysée Palace?

4

Who lives in the Vatican?

5

Where is the Kremlin?

6

In which city is the Great Hall of the People?

7

Whose headquarters are at Langley, Virginia?

8

Where does the UN General Assembly meet?

9

Which cities house the European Parliament?

10

In which city is the Palace of Westminster?

11

In which city does Canada's Parliament meet?

12

In which city does Australia's federal parliament meet?

POLITICS & POWER
SCANDALS

1

Which politician was linked to the Mary Jo Kopechne affair?

2

Which young woman almost brought Clinton down?

3

In which country was the Dreyfus scandal?

4

Where did the 1889 Panama Scandal erupt?

5

Which office did Spiro Agnew resign?

6

The 1974 movie about Watergate?

7

Where was Tammany Hall?

8

What were WMDs, not found in Iraq?

9

In which city was the Watergate building?

10

Name the two *Washington Post* journalists who exposed Watergate?

11

Which senator led a "communist witchhunt"?

12

The Teapot Dome was a scandal (1927); about what?

BALLOT
BOX

1

19th-Century. British explorer of Arabia who translated the *Kama Sutra*?

2

Where was the Weimar Republic?

3

What was President Coolidge's first name?

4

What "first" did Geraldine Ferraro achieve?

5

What happened on the battleship *Potemkin*?

6

In which city did the 1871 Communards take to the streets?

7

Nickname of Haiti's dictator Duvalier?

8

Which American university was founded in 1701?

9

Which famous American lived at Mount Vernon?

10

Where was Farouk king?

11

Which Polish prime minister was a famous pianist?

12

What was President Eisenhower's favorite sport?

POLITICS & POWER
ASSASSINATIONS

1

Who was stabbed in the Roman Senate in 44 BC?

2

Where were the Black Dragons brutal?

3

Who shot Abraham Lincoln in 1865?

4

Who did Sirhan Sirhan shoot in 1968?

5

Who was shot by James Earl Ray, also in 1968?

6

Which Russian monk was sentenced to death in 1916?

7

Which Egyptian leader was shot in 1981?

8

Which terror group killed Aldo Moro, 1978?

9

How was Alexander II of Russia killed in 1881?

10

Who was killed by Nathuram Godse in 1948?

11

Which British royal was blown up in a boat by the IRA, 1979?

12

Whom did Mark David Chapman shoot in 1980?

BALLOT
BOX

1

Why did some warships have rams?

2

What was a galleass?

3

Who went to war in longships?

4

Why did medieval ships have "castles"?

5

In which war was the Battle of the Coral Sea?

6

Who commanded the English fleet against the Armada?

7

Which US ship outfought the *Serapis* in 1779?

8

Which three nations fought at Trafalgar in 1805?

9

Which 1906 battleship made the rest obsolete?

10

Which battleship was scuttled at Montevideo, 1939?

11

Which navy lost the battleship *Hiei* in 1942?

12

What was Polaris?

1

What was Operation Dragoon in 1944?

2

What was an Unterseeboot?

3

Which wartime campaign was code-named TORCH?

4

Which leader promised "Victory, victory at all costs"?

5

What kind of craft was USS *Yorktown*?

6

What was a P-51?

7

In which group of islands is Guadalcanal?

8

In which theater of war did Merrill's Marauders operate?

9

What did a GI do with a BAR?

10

What fierce name had the German Panzer VI tank?

11

Which battle began in the Ardennes in December 1944?

12

Who commanded the US fleet at Leyte Gulf (October 1944)?

1

Which country conquered Guatemala in the 1500s?

2

Which Asian country did US-led NATO forces invade in 2001?

3

Who led his army to the gates of Vienna in 1529?

4

Which invasion was code-named Overlord?

5

What year did US forces remove Saddam Hussein from power in Iraq?

6

Where did Napoleon invade in 1812?

7

What did Philip of Spain send to England in 1588?

8

What was Operation Sealion?

9

Which Scandinavian invaders attacked England in the AD 800s?

10

Which nation invaded China in 1937?

11

Which Central Power did Russian general Brusilov's army attack
in June 1916?

12

Which Caribbean island did US forces invade in 1983?

WARS & WARFARE
MILITARY MISCELLANY (1)

1

Which British World War II airplane did R.J. Mitchell design?

2

What was Operation Barbarossa?

3

Who led the USAAF band until his disappearance in 1944?

4

What kind of ships were *Arizona* and *Warspite*?

5

What were "Ruperts"?

6

Who was David McCampbell?

7

Who joined Eagle squadrons?

8

What was *Tirpitz*?

9

Who was the pilot of B-29 *Enola Gay* (August 6, 1945)?

10

What did the letters ARP stand for?

11

Where did Tito lead anti-Nazi resistance fighters during World War II?

12

Where did Lt Annie Fox win a Purple Heart in 1941?

. . . .

1

What was World War II General Bradley's first name?

. . . .

2

In which military arm did Napoleon start his career?

. . . .

3

Who was Allied supreme commander on D-Day, 1944?

. . . .

4

Who was Rodrigo Diaz, hero of Spain?

. . . .

5

Which ex-pilot commanded the Luftwaffe in 1939?

. . . .

6

Which World War II general was played on screen (1970)
by George C. Scott?

. . . .

7

Whose nickname was "Stormin' Norman"?

. . . .

8

Who commanded the British Army in France from 1915?

. . . .

9

Who was General Giap?

. . . .

10

Which German general was known as the Desert Fox?

. . . .

11

Whom did Ney, Murat, and Bernadotte follow?

. . . .

12

Who commanded the Confederate army at Gettysburg ?

. . . .

WARS & WARFARE
FORTS AND CASTLES

1

Which fort on the Chicago River was built in 1803 by John Whistler?

2

What was the key feature of a concentric castle?

3

Who built castles called alcazars in Spain?

4

What was a portcullis?

5

In which country did daimyos build castles?

6

Which people built the fortress of Sacsayhuaman?

7

In which country is the fortress of Golconda?

8

For which French king did Vauban build fortifications?

9

What happened in a siege?

10

What were gabions (useful in sieges)?

11

What did sappers do?

12

Who built Fort Necessity in 1754 (in Pennsylvania)?

1

In which war was the Battle for Inchon?

2

Where was the Battle of Dien Bien Phu?

3

Where did Sandinistas fight Somoza?

4

Which two Middle Eastern countries went to war in 1980?

5

Which Middle East war was fought in 1967?

6

Where in Asia did 1971 civil war lead to partition?

7

Which European state invaded Abyssinia in 1935?

8

Which Arab country did Iraq invade in 1990?

9

In which war was the Tet Offensive?

10

Who launched the Tet Offensive?

11

What name was given to the 1973 Arab-Israeli war?

12

Why did Britain and Argentina go to war in 1982?

WARS & WARFARE
LOSERS

1

Who lost at Adrianople in AD 376?

2

In which 1863 battle in Georgia did Bragg's success leave
Rosecrans trapped?

3

Whose ships went down at Salamis?

4

Whose fleet was defeated at the Coral Sea in 1942?

5

Who lost at Valmy in 1792?

6

Who were defeated at Sedan in 1870?

7

Whose fleet came out worst at Tsushima (1905)?

8

Who lost at Crécy in 1346?

9

And who was defeated at Orléans in 1429?

10

Which general lost Quebec in 1759?

11

Which US regiment lost in 1876 at the Battle of Little Bighorn?

12

Who lost the Battle of Bunker Hill in 1775?

1

Which nation won its war with Spain, April-August 1898?

2

Who came out on top at Austerlitz in 1805?

3

Who triumphed at Poltava in 1709?

4

Where did Blucher turn up just in time?

5

Which Roman leader triumphed over Antony and Cleopatra at Actium?

6

Who was known as "The Liberator"?

7

Which Mongol conqueror was called the "wrath of God"?

8

Who defeated the Persians at Gaugamela?

9

Which future president won the Battle of Tippecanoe in 1811?

10

Who won for Britain in the Peninsular War?

11

Who led 16 bombers to Tokyo in April 1942?

12

Who commanded the US Pacific Fleet at Midway?

1

Who was the victor at Waterloo in 1815?

2

Who surrendered at Saratoga in 1777?

3

And which general surrendered at Yorktown in 1781?

4

Who defeated the Prussians at Jena in 1806?

5

At which battle was Stonewall Jackson killed in 1863?

6

Who commanded the US 1st Army, Normandy 1944?

7

Which army did Marshal Zhukov lead?

8

Which World War II general was nicknamed "Vinegar Joe"?

9

For what military actions was Civil War general Nathan Forrest famous?

10

Where did General McChrystal take over in 2009?

11

In which war did Ludendorff command?

12

Who led the Inchon landing in 1950?

1

What was the first Gatling gun?

2

And how did it work?

3

What was the Lee-Enfield?

4

What did lancers carry?

5

Who used sabers?

6

What was a scimitar?

7

What was a culverin?

8

What did a Roman do with his pilum?

9

Which fired farthest, a crossbow or longbow?

10

What were halberds?

11

Why did musketeers carry a smouldering match?

12

What may have originated at Bayonne, France in 1640?

1

What was a morion?

2

Where did a medieval knight wear greaves?

3

What did a knight hold in the couched position?

4

What was a knight's surcoat?

5

Which weapon fired bolts or quarrels?

6

What kind of weapon had a basket hilt?

7

What was a bazooka?

8

What was a Brown Bess?

9

From which end was a musket loaded?

10

What did an archer keep in his quiver?

11

What was Greek Fire?

12

What was a trebuchet used for?

WARS & WARFARE
ON THE MARCH

1

In which battle was Pickett's Charge?

2

In which battle was Hougoumont a key position?

3

Who used the "testudo" (tortoise) formation?

4

What was a "pull-through" used for?

5

What in World War II was a DUKW?

6

In Normandy 1944 what was an LCT?

7

What was a war hammer used for?

8

When did soldiers in Europe first wear uniforms?

9

In ancient warfare, what was a phalanx?

10

How many wheels had a Celtic chariot?

11

Where was a knight's visor?

12

Where were vambraces, on a suit of armor?

1

Where did samurai go to war?

2

Of what were Ancient Egyptian swords made?

3

Which large animals did Hannibal take to battle?

4

What were triremes?

5

Which two European countries fought at Agincourt in 1415?

6

Which country's navy used U-boats?

7

Where did Pheidippides run in 490 BC?

8

What kind of sea-craft was *Holland* (1898)?

9

Who led 1000 red shirts against Austria?

10

Where did George Custer and his men die, 1876?

11

What shape was a Viking shield?

12

Did a Norman wear chain mail or plate armor?

1

What year did World War I in Europe begin?

2

Which new weapon appeared in 1916?

3

Which was the biggest sea battle of the war?

4

Against whom did the Allies fight at Gallipoli?

5

What were Zeppelins?

6

What kind of weapon was a Lewis?

7

What were Pups and Camels?

8

Which Western Front hill has resonance for Canada?

9

What did the letters AEF stand for?

10

How were fascines used?

11

What were Q-ships?

12

Who was the Red Baron?

1

Who was "Black Jack," in Europe from 1917?

2

During which battle was poison gas first used?

3

Where was Austria's Archduke assassinated in 1914?

4

Where were angels said to be seen in the sky?

5

What new weapon was carried by HMS *Ark Royal*?

6

Remembrance Day (UK) is called what in the US?

7

What do the letters ANZAC stand for?

8

Which fortress did the French defend in 1916?

9

What blew up at Messines in 1917?

10

Where was No Man's Land?

11

What was phosgene?

12

Where did von Lettow-Vorbeck fight his war?

1

What were Shermans and Grants?

2

What was a Molotov cocktail?

3

What was a Stuka?

4

What was an "88"?

5

What were *Lexington* and *Wasp*?

6

What were Hellcats and Wildcats?

7

What was the normal crew of a German V-1?

8

What kind of weapons were X-craft?

9

On which US warship did the Japanese surrender?

10

What was the US M-1?

11

Which piece of a GI's equipment weighed 1lb (450g)?

12

What were Liberators and Flying Fortresses?

WARS & WARFARE
WORLD WAR II (2)

1

Where was the Vichy government?

2

What did Schutzstaffel (SS) mean in German?

3

Where did the Maquis resist the Nazis?

4

Who was the US Navy's first Fleet Admiral (1944)?

5

What was "window"?

6

Which island won the Victoria Cross for it heroism?

7

Where was Clark Field?

8

What were Enigma machines used for?

9

What were Waves and Wrens?

10

What branch of the military did General Carl Spaatz command?

11

What was Spaatz's nickname?

12

Where did Paulus surrender in January 1943?

1

Who led a raid at Harpers Ferry, 1859?

2

Which South Carolina target did Confederates attack in 1861?

3

On which side was Longstreet a general?

4

What were *zouaves*?

5

Which side lost the Battle of Fredericksburg, 1862?

6

Which general led a march through Georgia, 1864?

7

Which July 1863 battle was a turning point in the war?

8

What color were Confederate uniforms?

9

Who commanded Union troops at Shiloh, 1862?

10

At which city-battle did Thomas defeat Hood in December 1864?

11

What was Andersonville?

12

What happened to Henry Wirz, in charge there?

WARS & WARFARE
ANCIENT BATTLES

....

1

Who killed Hector outside Troy?

....

2

Which king died at Gilboa, about 1000 BC?

....

3

Where did 300 Spartans die in 480 BC?

....

4

And who was their leader?

....

5

Which Macedonian conquered Greece, 330s BC?

....

6

Who defeated Darius of Persia at Arbela?

....

7

What happened to the Romans at Lake Trasimene (217 BC)?

....

8

Who revolted in the so-called "Servile Wars"?

....

9

And who was their most famous leader?

....

10

Who won the Battle of Pharsalia (48 BC)?

....

11

Who lost at Philippi in 42 BC?

....

12

And who vanquished them?

....

WARS & WARFARE
OLD TIME WARS

. . . .

1

Which animals accompanied Hannibal crossing the Alps?

2

Which two opposing generals were each born in 1769?

3

What year was the Battle of Lepanto?

4

And was this battle fought on sea or on land?

5

Where was the Battle of Plassey (1757)?

6

In which century was King Philip's War?

7

Which three-day battle was fought in 1813?

8

In which war was the Battle of Tannenberg?

9

Where was the Battle of Novara in 1513?

10

Who did Pontiac lead to war in 1763?

11

On which continent was the Thirty Years' War fought?

12

Who beat the Swedes at the Battle of Neva, 1240?

1

Where was ANZAC cove?

2

In which country was the battle of Caporetto fought?

3

What was the name of the twin engine German bombing planes?

4

How did the *Lusitania* sink in May 1915?

5

In 1914, which nation had the largest navy?

6

And which country had the biggest army?

7

Which holy city did Britain's General Allenby enter, December 1917?

8

Complete the song title: *Keep the Home* ...

9

Who led the Arab Revolt in 1916?

10

Against whom were the Arabs fighting?

11

In what vehicle did French and Germans meet to discuss peace terms in 1918?

12

What was the AEF?

WARS & WARFARE
WHO WON?

1

The Abyssinian War, 1935-36?

2

The Hundred Years' War, 1337-1453?

3

The Anglo-Norman War, 1066?

4

The Russo-Japanese war, 1904-05?

5

The Spanish-American war, 1898?

6

The Wars of the Roses?

7

The Boer War, 1899-1902?

8

The Punic Wars (BC)?

9

The Seven Years' War 1756-63?

10

The American War of Independence, 1775-83?

11

The Sino-Japanese War, 1894-95?

12

Indo-Chinese war, 1945-54?

1

What happened to HMS *Prince of Wales* in 1942?

2

Which country leased 50 old destroyers to Britain?

3

Which admiral masterminded the Pearl Harbor attack?

4

How did this admiral die in April 1943?

5

What was special about the Me-262?

6

What does the German term "blitzkrieg" mean?

7

What was the Zero, new in July 1940?

8

Who were the Flying Tigers?

9

What was Operation Market Garden, 1944?

10

What was the iconic US woman riveter's name?

11

Which dictator's troops invaded Greece from Albania in October 1940?

12

What were Tigers and Panthers?

1

What was Peenemunde?

2

In which war was Nathan Hale hanged as a spy?

3

What did OSS stand for?

4

What was an Enigma machine used for?

5

Where was Soviet spy Richard Sorge based?

6

What were carrier pigeons used for?

7

Who was Cicero?

8

Who was in charge of Nazi propaganda?

9

What was the nationality of Mata Hari, executed by firing squad for espionage during World War I?

10

Who were the Rosenbergs?

11

For whom did Karl Schulmeister spy?

12

Who said one spy was worth 20,000 men?

1

What century was King Philip's War?

2

Who was King Philip?

3

In which war did the Iroquois side with the British?

4

Which war broke out in 1763 in the Ohio Valley?

5

Of whom was Tecumseh chief?

6

Who was "The Prophet"?

7

Whose victory at Tippecanoe (1811) sent him to the White House?

8

Where were the Seminole wars (1817-30s)?

9

Which people did Red Cloud and Crazy Horse lead?

10

Whom did Chief Joseph lead?

11

Which Apache leader finally surrendered in 1886?

12

Which Indian leader was killed at Standing Rock Reservation, 1890?

1

Which war did Matthew Brady photograph?

2

Who was Richard Harding Davis?

3

Which American broadcaster memorably reported on the London Blitz?

4

What did Pattle, Hartmann, and Bong have in common?

5

Which war was most costly in money terms?

6

Which war lasted from 1957 to 1975?

7

On which war did Peter Arnett and John Simpson report in 1991?

8

Which ex-Nazi was kidnapped in Argentina (1960)?

9

And what happened to him?

10

For what 1968 offense was Lt W. Calley punished?

11

Where did the World War II war crimes court sit?

12

Who declared war "on terror" in 2001?

1

In which war zone was Bagram base?

2

Which ship was nicknamed "the Great White Whale"?

3

What is a Harrier?

4

On which Japanese island did US troops land 19 February 1945?

5

Where was US flier James Jabara the first jet "ace"?

6

Which US facility on Cuba attracted attention post 9/11?

7

Whose troops moved into Afghanistan in 1979?

8

In which European war did NATO fight in the 1990s?

9

What post did Henry L. Stimson hold in World War II?

10

Who or what was Agent Orange?

11

Which rules provide for humane treatment of POWs?

12

Where was the Atlantic Wall?

1

What was the millennium bug?

2

What happened to "Arkan"?

3

Where was Hugo Chavez made president?

4

Whose independence did the PKK seek?

5

What was circling Eros?

6

What title did Michelle Kwan win?

7

Who won their third consecutive World Series title by defeating the Mets?

8

Who became the first president to address the Russian Parliament?

9

President Assad died June 10, 2000; where had he ruled?

10

Where did a government ban poppy-growing?

11

In which new state were there riots in Kupang?

12

Who won his third election in Canada?

. . . .

1

What did the Shoemakers and Levy discover in 1993?

. . . .

2

Which first lady joined the Senate?

. . . .

3

What job did John Bolton take on in 2005?

. . . .

4

Who was Ben Bernanke?

. . . .

5

Whose play *The History Boys* won awards?

. . . .

6

Which movie star became governor of California?

. . . .

7

Which Irish actor made his Bond debut in *GoldenEye*?

. . . .

8

What date were the 2005 terror attacks in London?

. . . .

9

What had been announced the previous day?

. . . .

10

Where was Recep Tayyip Erdogan prime minister?

. . . .

11

Who is Knut, drawing crowds?

. . . .

12

Who succeeded Tony Blair as British prime minister?

. . . .

1

Daw Aung San Suu Kyi

2

Bob Dole

3

Sani Abacha

4

Suharto

5

Eduard Shevardnadze

6

Paul Keating

7

Haris Slajdzic

8

Wei Jingsheng

9

Fidel Ramos

10

Hastings Banda

11

Queen Margrethe II

12

Hojatolislam Rafsanjani

1

What was the nickname of I. Lewis Libby?

2

Which Internet service provider was headed by Steve Case?

3

Where did President Hafez al-Assad hold power?

4

Who was Walter Matthau?

5

Which Canadian politician died in September 2000?

6

Who released *The Marshall Mathers* LP?

7

In which country was President Obama's father born?

8

What are Fannie Mae and Freddie Mac known for selling?

9

What office did Henry Paulson hold in 2008?

10

Where was Alexander Litvinenko killed?

11

Who won an Oscar for being Daniel Plainview?

12

Which former president died December 26, 2006?

1

Which Panama leader gave himself up?

2

Which country said "goodbye" to Samuel Doe?

3

Where was Li Peng in charge?

4

Which Soviet republic's capital was Vilnius?

5

Which Russian was trying to hold things together?

6

In which Soviet republic did violence erupt in Baku?

7

Which Bulgarian leader ended up in jail?

8

Who was South Africa's president?

9

And who did he free from jail?

10

Where was Vaclav Havel president?

11

Where were the Sandinistas voted out?

12

Where was Juan Ponce Enrile arrested?

MODERN TIMES
THE GULF WAR

1

What invasion started the Gulf War in August 1990?

2

What was the prize?

3

Who ordered the invasion?

4

Which country sent the Daguet Division to war?

5

Which army used its Republican Guard?

6

What were Scuds?

7

What were Patriots?

8

What was the code name for the Allied operation?

9

Six took part; what were they?

10

What was the *Missouri*?

11

To which country did many Iraqi planes escape?

12

Who was US president at the time of the war?

1

Which African state did the US bomb in 1986?

2

President Samora Michel died in a plane crash 1986; where had he ruled?

3

Who succeeded his assassinated mother as India's leader?

4

What did OPEC cut in 1983?

5

Which Australian actor starred in the movie *The River*?

6

Which president died in a 1988 plane crash?

7

Who won a 1988 Pulitzer Prize for her novel *Beloved*?

8

Where was Habib Bourguiba ousted?

9

What award was given to Desmond Tutu?

10

Which animated movie star quacked past 50 in 1984?

11

Which African state did Cuban troops leave?

12

Who was shot in St Peter's Square (1981)?

1

Author of *A Man For All Seasons*

2

British comedian, often worked with Dudley Moore

3

Mother of JFK

4

Champion of the "little black dress"

5

Danced with Fred Astaire in the 1930s

6

First Lady, who remarried to a Greek shipping magnate

7

Lead singer with Nirvana, died 1994

8

1940s Hollywood "sweater girl"

9

Co-inventor of ENIAC, the first computer

10

Singing sister of Patty and LaVerne

11

American female runner, won 3 sprint golds at the Rome Olympics

12

Tennis star, known to his fans as "Pancho"

1

For what did *Lionheart* challenge in 1980?

2

What did Robert Ballard find underwater?

3

Which Swedish-born Hollywood star died in 1982?

4

Site of a serious nuclear accident in the USSR?

5

What was the name of the first US Space Shuttle?

6

Who said in March 1981 "Honey, I forgot to duck"?

7

What fate had he just avoided?

8

Where were ZANLA and ZIPRA fighting one another?

9

Where was Isabel Peron jailed for corruption?

10

Which country staged Expo 86?

11

Where was Terry Waite kidnapped?

12

Brian M..., prime minister of Canada?

1

Who was Vito Genovese?

2

In what game was Boris Spassky a champion?

3

Who became premier of France in 1962?

4

Of which state was Nelson Rockefeller governor?

5

Civil Rights activist, who strove to enter Mississippi University?

6

Which country was led by Norman Manley?

7

What did Alan Dulles head until 1961?

8

Which candidates debated on TV in 1960?

9

Where was U Thant the new man in 1961?

10

Rock band with whom Brian Jones played?

11

Actor who played detective Virgil Tibbs on screen?

12

Who took over from Jack Paar in 1962?

MODERN TIMES
MORE 1960s STUFF

1

What year was the Cuban missile crisis?

2

In which country was Andropov laid to rest?

3

What was the B-1B?

4

Which writer published *God Knows*?

5

Who was shot in the Ambassador Hotel, Los Angeles?

6

Where did Novotny resign?

7

Where did Marines land in 1965?

8

Where was the Bay of Pigs?

9

In which European city did the death of Jan Palach cause uproar?

10

Whom did Jack Ruby shoot?

11

What was the PLO?

12

Which jazz great fingered his last keys in 1984?

MODERN TIMES
MORE 1980s

1

What were "Cabbage Patch" items in toyshops?

2

Ansel Adams died in 1984: for what was he famous?

3

Name the only state won by Walter Mondale in the 1984 election.

4

What post did Jeane Kirkpatrick hold 1981-84?

5

Who won his fifth British Open golf title in 1983?

6

Which dead dictator's daughter went home in 1984?

7

Died 1987, said "everyone will be famous for 15 minutes"?

8

Which sport's World Cup finals were held in Mexico, 1986?

9

Real name Richard Jenkins, died 1984. Who was he?

10

Which Nobel prize did Elias Canetti win in 1981?

11

For whom was Larry Speakes a spokesperson?

12

Who bossed News International?

1

Where was Marshal Voroshilov head of state?

2

Which dam on the Zambezi opened in 1960?

3

What state did Senator John Kennedy represent?

4

What was the *France*?

5

Which Hitchcock film put Anthony Perkins into drag?

6

Which iconic singer left the US Army?

7

What happened to Gary Powers' U-2?

8

Who told little Susie to wake up?

9

Who won his first pro fight in his hometown of Louisville?

10

From which country was Nobel Peace prize winner Albert Luthuli?

11

Whose widow was Kay Spreckles?

12

Who banged the desk with his shoe at the UN?

MODERN TIMES

LEADERS IN 1999...OF WHERE?

1

President Havel

2

Prime Minister Jospin

3

Prime Minister Bandaranaike

4

Prime Minister Mitchell

5

Prime Minister Kok

6

President Kim Dae Jung

7

President Saddam Hussein

8

Prime Minister Vajpayee

9

President McAleese

10

Prime Minister Obuchi

11

President Muluzi

12

Prime Minister Chrétien

MODERN TIMES
1990s EVENTS

1
What did the initials CIS stand for?

2
Which three states set it up in 1991?

3
Which CIS state controlled its nuclear weapons?

4
Who was Russia's most popular politician in 1991?

5
Where was Edith Cresson a leading politician?

6
Which state's capital was Monrovia?

7
Which state gave the King Faisal International Prize?

8
Where did the Lombard League campaign?

9
What was Hans Blick looking for in Iraq?

10
Where was Bhumibol king?

11
Who was the last British governor of Hong Kong?

12
What year did Britain hand back Hong Kong to China?

MODERN TIMES
MORE FROM THE 1990s

1

Where was Yoweri Museveni president?

2

For what trade was the "Golden Triangle" notorious?

3

Where did Jorgé Sampaio become president in 1996?

4

Which African king died in a car accident in 1996?

5

Where did peasants revolt in Chiapas state?

6

Where was Najibullah deposed in 1992?

7

What year did Slovakia become independent?

8

Where was Operation Restore Hope ?

9

To which island did Aristide return in 1994?

10

Where was the Armed Islamic Group (GIA) active?

11

Where did UNITA fight a war?

12

Where did Helmut Kohl still head the government in 1994 after
12 years?

MODERN TIMES
THE 1970s

1

Where did Yakubu Gowon head the government?

2

Which organization won the 1977 Nobel peace prize?

3

Which country invaded northern Cyprus?

4

Into where did Moroccans go on the Green March?

5

Which poet (noted for her hats) died in 1972?

6

Who became Secretary of State in 1973?

7

Where were the "Four Modernizations"?

8

When did Ireland join the European Community?

9

Where did Flt Lt Jerry Rawlings seize power in 1979?

10

Which new US airliner entered service in 1970?

11

From which British university did Prince Charles graduate, 1970?

12

Why did the stage show *Oh! Calcutta!* arouse comment?

MODERN TIMES
1970s NEWSMAKERS

1

In which Washington scandal was H. R. Haldeman involved?

2

Which Spanish leader died in 1975?

3

Who was Oleg Protopopov?

4

Who was Andrey Gromyko?

5

Where was Dawson's Field?

6

And what happened at Dawson's Field in 1970?

7

J. Edgar Hoover died in 1972; who was he?

8

What was the Tu-144, which crashed in Paris in 1973?

9

Where did Ernesto Geisel become president, 1974?

10

Which foreign monarch toured the US in July 1976?

11

Which British duo created the stage hit *Jesus Christ Superstar*?

12

Where was ex-premier Bhutto executed in 1979?

1

Where was the Bar-Lev Line?

2

In 1973 Native Americans took over this historic site.

3

What TV program was called *All in the Family* in the UK?

4

Who was prime minister of Israel in 1970?

5

Who succeeded Spiro Agnew as US Vice President?

6

Which German rocket pioneer died in June 1977?

7

How was Georgi Markov killed in 1978?

8

Who met Jimmy Carter at Camp David in 1978?

9

In which Asian country was Zahir Shah deposed as king in 1973?

10

Who was the defeated Democrat in the 1972 US election?

11

Where did Constantine Karamanlis return in 1974?

12

Which prima donna bowed out in 1977?

1

When was Reagan first elected president?

2

Which party's candidate was he?

3

Whom did he defeat?

4

His childhood nickname?

5

The most-quoted line from his film career?

6

Who was his First Lady?

7

Where was he governor 1966-75?

8

Who was Reagan's choice as vice president?

9

To which Caribbean island did Reagan send troops in 1983?

10

Which musicians did the Reagans restore to the White House?

11

When did Reagan begin his second term?

12

Whom did he defeat to win it?

1

Indian politician Rajiv?

2

Supreme Court judge Sandra Day?

3

Olympic gymnast Mary Lou?

4

American choreographer Martha?

5

Soviet scientist/human rights activist Andrey?

6

Chile's President Augusto?

7

Aussie movie star Mel?

8

Alexander, US Secretary of State?

9

Orchestral conductor Herbert von?

10

Rev Jesse?

11

1984 Los Angeles Olympic boss Peter V.?

12

British actor Jeremy who played Claus Von Bulow in 1990?

1

In which church was Archbishop Lefebvre a rebel?

2

In which stage show did Michael Crawford wear a mask?

3

Author of *In Cold Blood*, he died 1984?

4

Mozambique's first president, died 1986?

5

Escaped assassination in Tripoli in 1984?

6

Bette D, actress, died 1989?

7

Where did Jaruzelski arrive in power (1981)?

8

Where was Nimeiry head of state?

9

Where did Kim Chong Il become next in line?

10

Governor of New York City 1983?

11

François M, President of France?

12

Whose hair caught fire while filming a commercial (1984)?

119

MODERN TIMES
1980s AND 1990s TRIVIA

1

Who was Yelena Bonner's famous husband?

2

In what affair was Ollie North a central figure?

3

By what name was Theodor Seuss Geisel popularly known?

4

What post did Kofi Annan hold?

5

Where was Mount Pinatubo?

6

For what was Naomi Uemura celebrated?

7

Who sang *I Heard It Through The Grapevine* (died in 1984)?

8

And how did this singer die?

9

What did the USS *Vincennes* shoot down (1988)?

10

Where did Jacques Chirac become prime minister in 1986?

11

Hasbro bought Tonka in 1991; what did it make?

12

Where was Paola queen?

1

Where did Colonel Boumedienne seize power in 1965?

2

Where was Hosni Mubarak a long-serving leader?

3

What did Courrèges design?

4

Singer with Nirvana, died 1994; who was he?

5

Who referred to "my fellow citizens" in January 1961?

6

What formal wear did he revert to for the ceremony?

7

Where did Lal Shastri become top man in 1964?

8

Which veteran anti-Communist died in Taipei, 1975?

9

Where did Noureddine Morceli do his moving?

10

Which office did Gary Hart have his eye on?

11

Who was Wilt the Stilt, died in 1999?

12

Who married Bianca in 1971?

ADVENTURE & EXPLORATION
PIRATES

1

What were privateers?

2

What was Bartholomew Roberts' nickname?

3

What's a common nickname for the pirate black flag?

4

Which classic novel features the character Long John Silver?

5

Which pirate sailed the *Adventure Galley*?

6

How might captured women pirates hope to escape hanging?

7

Where did Barbary corsairs roam?

8

Which Indian Ocean island was a pirate HQ?

9

Which pirate was shot dead off Carolina in 1718?

10

Which pirate became deputy governor of Jamaica?

11

Which pirate refused to attack New Orleans in 1814?

12

Which modern-day African state is notorious for offshore piracy?

ADVENTURE & EXPLORATION
EXPLORING AFRICA

1

Which river did Mungo Park explore?

2

What was James Bruce looking for in Ethiopia?

3

Who was Burton's explorer-companion in Africa?

4

Which lake did this explorer name?

5

Who was the first European to cross Africa, 1854-56?

6

Which river did he follow?

7

Which newspaper sent H. M. Stanley to Africa?

8

What was the object of Stanley's journey?

9

Near which lake did Stanley and Livingston meet?

10

Which river in West Africa did Stanley explore?

11

Which pair of explorers did Samuel Baker meet in 1863?

12

Which Europeans led the exploration of the Sahara?

1

Where did Bougainville explore?

2

What was the name of Columbus' flagship?

3

How many ships made up his fleet?

4

John Cabot sailed for England, but what nationality was he?

5

Where did Pinzon and Cabral sail?

6

With whom had Pinzon sailed previously?

7

Who founded Québec in 1608?

8

What did Balboa see in 1513?

9

And what had he just accomplished?

10

For what did sailors use an astrolabe?

11

How many voyages did Henry the Navigator make?

1 2

In which continent was the fabled kingdom of Prester John?

1

Who coined the phrase "New World"?

2

Where did Ponce de Leon explore from 1513?

3

What was Hernando De Soto looking for?

4

And where did he seek it?

5

Which river did the De Soto expedition reach?

6

Where were the Seven Cities of Cibola said to be?

7

Which Spaniard went looking for them in 1540?

8

What was Verrazano sent to find in 1524?

9

Which region did he explore?

10

Which English courtier is said to have brought tobacco to England
from America?

11

Who gave his name to the strait between Greenland and Canada?

12

Which American animal most interested Europeans?

ADVENTURE & EXPLORATION
WHERE DID THEY EXPLORE?

1

Willem Jansz (Holland) early 1600s?

2

Abel Janszoon Tasman (Holland)?

3

Louis Jolliet and Jacques Marquette (France) 1600s?

4

Henry Hudson (England) early 1600s?

5

Lewis and Clark (USA) early 1800s?

6

Vitus Bering (Denmark) 1700s?

7

Samuel and Florence Baker (Britain) 1800s?

8

William Edward Parry (Britain) 1800s?

9

James Cook (Britain) 1700s?

10

Richard E. Byrd (USA) 1920s?

11

Charles Wilkes (USA) 1840s?

12

Vivian Fuchs (Britain) 1950s?

ADVENTURE & EXPLORATION
ANCIENT EXPLORERS

1

Who sailed the Red Sea to Punt?

2

Who first landed in New Zealand?

3

Where did Hanno of Carthage explore?

4

Which islands did Pytheas sail round?

5

Where did Ptolemy the geographer live?

6

Why did mariners of old fear mermaids?

7

Who was Ibn Batuta?

8

Where did Cheng Ho lead a fleet?

9

Which people discovered Iceland about 870?

10

Which island did Eric the Red explore?

11

Where was Vinland?

12

And who named it?

1

Where did Henry the Navigator live?

2

What was a cross-staff?

3

What was a caravel?

4

Which island did the Portuguese reach in 1419?

5

What southerly point did Diaz first see?

6

Who left Portugal for India in 1497?

7

What role did Ibn Majid play in this voyage?

8

Who set sail around the world in 1519?

9

How many ships began the voyage?

10

And from which country?

11

Where was the expedition leader killed?

12

And how many ships returned home?

ADVENTURE & EXPLORATION
BRAVE SAILORS

....

1

Who sailed in the *Gjoa* in 1903-06?

....

2

And what passage did he navigate?

....

3

After which explorer was Canada's biggest bay named?

....

4

From which European country did Samuel de Champlain hail?

....

5

Who was cast adrift by mutineers in 1787?

....

6

What did Blyth and Ridgway row across (1966)?

....

7

Who was Brendan the Navigator?

....

8

The first Englishman to sail around the world?

....

9

And the name of his ship?

....

10

The coast of which continent did sailor Charles Wilkes explore in 1840?

....

11

Who took *Fram* into the Arctic ice in 1895?

....

12

Where did Joshua Slocum sail 1895-98?

....

ADVENTURE & EXPLORATION
HIGH FLYERS

. . . .

1

Whose *Eole* "hopped" in 1890?

2

Which ocean did Alcock and Brown cross?

3

When did Concorde begin regular commercial flights into New York?

4

Of what aerial device were Leslie Irvin and Harold Harris 20th-century pioneers?

5

What is an ornithopter, as built by Lawrence Hargrave in the 1890s?

6

What is the Boeing 747 commonly known as?

7

Who was Bessie Coleman?

8

Who was the first woman to break the sound barrier?

9

Who invented the seaplane in 1911?

10

What first did Sally Ride achieve in 1983?

11

Who was first to fly the Atlantic solo?

12

And the year?

ADVENTURE & EXPLORATION
FLYING FEATS

1

Who flew over both North and South Poles?

2

In which US state was the first airplane flight, December 17, 1903?

3

Year of the first-ever balloon ascent by people?

4

Can you name either balloonist?

5

Which American was nicknamed the "Flying Deb"?

6

What feat did Jerrie Mock achieve?

7

What was the ballistic missile used by Germany during World War II?

8

Which ocean did Clyde Pangborn cross in 1931?

9

Where did Wiley Post fly in 1933?

10

Who flew the X-1 supersonic in 1947?

11

What kind of machine was the Bell Model 47 of 1945?

12

What feat did *Double Eagle 2* achieve in 1978?

ADVENTURE & EXPLORATION
AMELIA EARHART

1

What did Amelia Earhart do in 1932?

2

What organization did she found in 1929?

3

Where did Earhart start her 1932 flight?

4

And where did she land?

5

What was her aircraft type?

6

How many people had flown the Atlantic solo before?

7

What food did Earhart take with her?

8

Why did she also carry smelling salts?

9

How long did her flight take?

10

In 1935, she made another solo flight...where?

11

What year did Earhart disappear?

12

What was she trying to do?

1

Whose *Aerodrome* fell into the Potomac?

2

What was the name of the Wrights' aircraft?

3

German glider pioneer, killed in 1896?

4

What flew less than 3ft (1m) high in 1907?

5

What nationality was Alberto Santos-Dumont?

6

What was the name of the plane he flew in 1906?

7

What was unusual about this plane (to modern eyes)?

8

Who started the first US airplane company in 1907?

9

Who was Charles Furnas?

10

With whom did Mrs van Deman fly in October 1909?

11

American engineer and glider pioneer (1832-1910)?

12

US businessman and plane-maker who bought TWA and built
the *Spruce Goose*?

ADVENTURE & EXPLORATION
UP, UP AND AWAY

1

First to demonstrate a hot air balloon?

2

First living creatures to fly in a balloon?

3

The world's first aeronaut?

4

And the date of his flight?

5

Why could he not go far?

6

Who did the French king say should make the flight?

7

When did women first go up in a balloon?

8

What did Blanchard try on a balloon in October 1784?

9

Did it work?

10

How were the first aeronauts killed?

11

Who made the first free balloon flight in the USA?

12

Who commanded the first US Army Balloon Corps (1861)?

ADVENTURE & EXPLORATION
FAMOUS EXPLORERS

1

Which river did Cartier sail up?

2

Who founded Montreal?

3

Which lakes did Robert de la Salle explore?

4

Swiss pioneer of bathyscaph exploration of the ocean deeps?

5

What did Burke and Wills die trying to cross?

6

Which continent did Humboldt explore?

7

With whom did Matthew Henson brave the cold?

8

Which English captain made three Pacific voyages?

9

Which explorer was set adrift by his own crew?

10

Who sailed a raft across the Pacific in 1947?

11

What was its name?

12

Where did Jan van Riebeeck found a base?

ADVENTURE & EXPLORATION
MORE FLYING FEATS

1

Who was the world's first woman pilot?

2

Who was the first person to die in a plane crash?

3

Who was piloting the plane at the time?

4

What did Eugene B. Ely do in 1910?

5

Who was Blanche Scott?

6

In which country was the first air collision?

7

What was the first item of air freight (1910)?

8

Who was Harriet Quimby?

9

And what first did she achieve in 1912?

10

Which two fliers claimed to have flown over the North Pole in 1926?

11

What did a US Navy NC-4 flying boat do in 1919?

12

Who first flew the Atlantic nonstop?

ADVENTURE & EXPLORATION
AMERICAN PIONEER LIFE

1

Which mountains did the first pioneers have to cross?

2

Which backwoodsman cut a trail across them?

3

How did pioneers travel the Ohio River?

4

What was "johnnycake"?

5

What vehicle was named for a valley in Pennsylvania?

6

What was a flatboat?

7

What was "chinking"?

8

What was a "house-raising"?

9

What was greased paper used for?

10

The basic ingredient of hominy is...?

11

What became the traditional bird at Thanksgiving?

12

What was linsey-woolsey?

1

Who tested the first liquid-fueled rocket (1936)?

2

Why did some scientists think space rockets wouldn't work?

3

Who was Herman Oberth?

4

Which German headed the US Army missile program?

5

What was the Vostok?

6

Who circled the earth on April 12, 1961?

7

How did he die in 1968?

8

Who flew in *Friendship* 7, 1962?

9

How many orbits did he make?

10

Who married fellow-cosmonaut Nikolayev?

11

The first astronaut to die during a mission?

12

What first did Aleksei Leonov mark up in 1965?

ADVENTURE & EXPLORATION
AMERICAN ASTRONAUTS

1

Who was the second American to fly in space?

2

By what nickname was he usually known?

3

What was significant about his *Gemini 3* trip?

4

How did he die in 1967?

5

Which other two astronauts died that day?

6

Who flew with Frank Borman in *Gemini 7*, 1965?

7

Where did they fly together again in 1968?

8

What was unlucky about *Apollo 13*?

9

Who commanded *Apollo 13*?

10

What was Neil Armstrong's first space mission?

11

Who were his two companions on *Apollo 11*?

12

And which of them landed on the Moon?

1

Who was William Clark's companion?

2

What was Clark's particular skill?

3

On what river did their journey begin in 1804?

4

Who was Sacagawea?

5

Who was J. C. Frémont?

6

Which famous scout guided him to Oregon?

7

Where did Jedediah Smith arrive in 1826?

8

Where did Stephen F. Austin settle?

9

Which battle won Texas its independence, 1836?

10

Where did the Old Spanish Trail end?

11

Where were (and are), the Badlands?

12

What were Santa Fé, Mormon, and Oregon?

ADVENTURE & EXPLORATION
MORE ABOUT THE WEST

1

For what was George Catlin best known?

2

Born 1786, Tennessee, died 1836. Who was he?

3

What was John Chapman's nickname?

4

And why was he given it?

5

What were pelts?

6

By whom was Daniel Boone captured in 1778?

7

And what Indian name was he given?

8

Who said he had killed 105 bears in seven months?

9

Which lake did Jim Bridger reach in 1824?

10

Which (modern) national park did he explore?

11

In which (modern) state did he build Fort Bridger?

12

Which trail did Bridger scout for gold-seekers?

1

Which frontiersman gave his name to a knife?

2

Who performed in the play *Scouts of the Prairie*?

3

Whose Wild West show became a hit?

4

How did Buffalo Bill acquire his name?

5

In which western town did Calamity Jane live?

6

Who was the most famous marshal of Tombstone?

7

Where was the gunfight at the OK Corral?

8

Henry McCarty became famous as...?

9

And who shot him in 1881?

10

Which outlaw was born in Clay Co., Missouri in 1847?

11

Who was his brother and accomplice?

12

Who said he was "the only law west of the Pecos"?

1

How many voyages did Columbus make?

2

Which country discovered Madagascar: Spain, Portugal or England?

3

Which river did De Solis discover in 1516?

4

Who gave the Pacific its name?

5

And why?

6

Who brought *Gypsy Moth* home in 1967?

7

And where had he sailed?

8

Where did *Endurance* sail in 1914?

9

And who led the expedition it carried?

10

For what did Willoughby and Chancellor look (1500s)?

11

Who first crossed the Antarctic Circle (1774)?

12

Who first set eyes on the Antarctic coast?

ADVENTURE & EXPLORATION
THE FIRST FLIERS

1

What were the Wright brothers' first names?

2

In which Ohio town did they live?

3

What was their father's occupation?

4

What toy may have inspired the brothers?

5

What business did the brothers open in 1892?

6

Which German glider pioneer caught their interest?

7

What did the Wrights begin flying in 1900?

8

Where did the brothers test their machines?

9

What year did the Wrights' first airplane fly?

10

Who was the pilot on the first flight?

11

How many people saw the historic flight?

12

Where did Wilbur take their plane in 1908?

ADVENTURE & EXPLORATION
LINDBERGH'S ADVENTURE

1

What did Lindbergh set out to do on May 20, 1927?

2

What year was Lindbergh born?

3

What did he become after school?

4

His next flying job, after the Army, was as...?

5

What did Raymond Orteig offer in 1919?

6

Which company built Lindbergh's plane?

7

What did Lindbergh name the plane?

8

How did he test it (May 10-11, 1927)?

9

How many engines did Lindbergh's plane have?

10

Why was looking out a problem?

11

Where did Lindbergh land?

12

How long did his epic flight last?

1

First to the South Pole in 1912?

2

First to set foot on the Moon?

3

Teenage diarist in hiding, she died in 1945?

4

Led South Africa to majority black rule?

5

Campaigned for civil rights in US until assassinated in 1965?

6

First runner to break four minutes for the mile?

7

First humans to stand atop Everest?

8

Soldier whose "Plan" revitalized post-war Europe?

9

Which 'Mother' won a Nobel Peace Prize?

10

Led Czech resistance to Soviets in 1968?

11

Russian exiled in 1974 for writing about the gulags?

12

Wartime and post-war leader of France?

1

Who was Philip of Macedon's famous son?

2

Which Greek state most admired physical strength?

3

What were Spartans famous for being slow at?

4

Who lost to the Greeks at Salamis?

5

Who became ruler of Greece at the age of 20 in 336 BC?

6

Who was the most famous pupil of Socrates?

7

Which king led the Greeks to Troy?

8

Whose face "launched a thousand ships"?

9

How did the Greeks enter Troy?

10

Which goddess rose from the sea near Cyprus?

11

Who sailed in the Argo?

12

And what did they seek?

1

Where was the Grand Canal built?

2

Who was born at Mecca in 570?

3

Who founded a monastery on Iona in 563?

4

What office did Gregory the Great hold 590-604?

5

Where was Suiko empress 593-628?

6

Who led a mission to Ireland in 432?

7

Which people did Gaiseric rule (400s)?

8

Which British king, legend says, ruled from Camelot?

9

Whose Goths sacked Rome?

10

Who led the Huns from 433-453?

11

Which empire did Belisarius fight for?

12

Where did Yezdigird the Wicked rule?

1

Independent from Portugal in 1975?

2

German from 1884, then Anglo-French?

3

Islands in Mozambique Channel, French until 1974?

4

Formerly the Afars and the Issas?

5

Embraced Christianity in the 4th century AD?

6

Here Libreville was founded in 1849?

7

Capital Banjul, independent from Britain 1965?

8

French in 1893, independent in 1960, capital Abidjan?

9

Nation founded by Moshoeshoe I in the 1820s?

10

Founded as a US-style republic in 1847?

11

Where Dr Hastings Banda was president?

12

Medieval empire, independent from France in 1960?

1

How did Jane Seymour die?

2

How were Elizabeth I and Mary Queen of Scots related?

3

Whom did Queen Elizabeth call "my little frog"?

4

What was sack?

5

What post did John Whitgift hold?

6

What were Dragon's Milk and Mad Dog?

7

Which playwright was also perhaps a spy?

8

Who died fighting on the *Revenge* in 1591?

9

Who were the Lord Chamberlain's Men?

10

Whose cottage is at Shottery, near Stratford?

11

Which Tudor monarch owned over 50 palaces?

12

Which father and son shaped Tudor policy?

1

Who took the Trail of Tears?

2

Who defeated Crook at the Rosebud?

3

Which Sioux group did Sitting Bull lead?

4

Which Oglala leader died in 1909, aged 87?

5

In which state was the 1864 Sand Creek Massacre?

6

What was a travois?

7

What was the main food-animal of Plains Indians?

8

What was "counting coup"?

9

What was "jerky"?

10

Who led the Chiricahua Apache until 1886?

11

What was The Ghost Dance?

12

What protection did it allegedly convey?

WORLD HISTORY 2
AMERICA IN THE 19TH CENTURY

1

Which president issued his Doctrine in 1823 ?

2

Which state joined the Union in 1821?

3

What year did the California Gold Rush begin?

4

Which president died after a month in office, 1841?

5

Who was the first president who'd been born in a log cabin?

6

What was confirmed by the 14th Amendment (1868)?

7

What year did Ulysses S. Grant become president?

8

In which industry did Andrew Carnegie get rich?

9

What year (post Civil War) did the last Federal troops leave the South?

10

Which four states joined the Union in 1889?

11

Who succeeded President Arthur in 1885?

12

What grew from 9,000 miles in 1850 to almost 200,000 miles in 1900?

1

Who were the Punic Wars between?

2

Who heroically defended the Tiber Bridge?

3

Who were the enemy?

4

Which animal, legend said, suckled Rome's founders?

5

Who crossed the Rubicon?

6

Who wrote a book about his Gallic wars?

7

What did Horace and Ovid do?

8

What did a "retiarius" fight with?

9

Who ran away from Octavia?

10

Who led the plot to kill Caesar?

11

What was a hypocaust?

12

Who or what were the plebs?

WORLD HISTORY 2
WAY OUT WEST

1

What was the Butterfield Line?

2

Who carried the mails and passengers from 1852?

3

Who rode from St Joseph on a pony on April 3, 1860?

4

What met at Promontory Point, May 10, 1869?

5

Which two companies achieved this meeting?

6

What were bullwhackers and muleskinners?

7

What was a "stern-wheeler"?

8

Why did locomotives have "cowcatchers"?

9

What was a Derringer?

10

Who was Annie Oakley?

11

Who killed Yellow Hand in 1876?

12

Who died holding the "dead man's hand"?

1

Why is this date celebrated by Americans?

2

What was the name of NASA's space probe that landed on Mars, 1997?

3

Work started on which canal in 1817?

4

Three US presidents died on this day. Who were they?

5

Who was the 30th president, born 1872?

6

Who was the Italian patriot, born this day 1807?

7

Which famous statue was handed over in 1884?

8

Which Pacific islands gained independence in 1946?

9

Who was the Polish leader, died in a plane crash in 1943?

10

Who did boxer Jess Willard lose to in 1919?

11

Who was the most famous woman scientist, died 1934?

12

Where did the first employment agency open, 1631?

155

WORLD HISTORY 2
IN WHICH CENTURY WAS...?

1

The Charge of the Light Brigade

2

The Alamo

3

The Fall of the Bastille

4

The Battle of Gallipoli

5

The Siege of Orléans

6

The Battle of Monte Cassino

7

The Battle of Roncesvalles

8

The Mongol conquest of China

9

The First Crusade

10

The Battle of Bull Run

11

The Battle of Bunker Hill

12

The battle of Manzikert

1

When did nine states including Ohio join the Union?

2

From whom did the US buy Louisiana?

3

What became the northern border of the US in 1818?

4

Which country ceded Florida to the US?

5

When was Texas annexed?

6

When did the US border first reach the Pacific?

7

From which country did the US buy California?

8

Which states came with the Gadsden Purchase, 1853?

9

Which territory was brought from Russia in 1867?

10

Which state was originally New Connecticut?

11

Which state is known as the Old Dominion?

12

Which is the Beehive State?

1

Which river made Egypt's civilization possible?

2

What was the "Black Land"?

3

What was the title of Egyptian kings?

4

What did the title originally mean?

5

Re or Ra was god of what?

6

Who was Bast?

7

What is Egyptian writing called?

8

Who was Hatshepsut?

9

What did Imhotep design at Saqqara?

10

What were put in canopic jars?

11

Where were shabti figures placed?

12

In what process was natron used?

WORLD HISTORY 2
THE YEAR 1776

1
What was the Marquis d'Abbans trying on the river?

2
Where was a statue of George III pulled down?

3
What name-change did Congress agree, September 9?

4
Which West-Coast city was founded by Spanish settlers?

5
Which society was founded at the College of William and Mary?

6
Who said July 4 should "be solemnized with pomp and parade"?

7
Who were Hessians?

8
Who set sail from England on his third voyage?

9
Who published the first volume of his history of Rome?

10
Who arrived in Paris to seek French aid for America?

11
Who composed his *Serenade in D*, for Elizabeth Haffner?

12
Which notorious writer went on the run (arrested February 1777)?

1

Whose flagship was *Revenge* in 1588?

2

Which English ship did the Dutch call "The Golden Devil"?

3

Who was known as "The Father of the American Navy"?

4

Which navies fought the Four Days' Battle (1666)?

5

Which ship fought the *Bonhomme Richard* in 1779?

6

Which is the oldest ship in the US Navy?

7

Why were gun-decks painted red?

8

Whose navy included the *Hancock* and the *Washington*?

9

Which two fleets fought at Chesapeake Bay in 1781?

10

And who won?

11

What was the name the world's first combat submarine, 1776?

12

Which English ship sailed to battle 1805 with 22 Americans on board?

1

What did rustlers steal?

2

What is a shaman?

3

What is a tepee?

4

What was a wickiup?

5

What is a chuck wagon?

6

In folktale, who had a giant ox named Babe?

7

How long did the Pony Express operate?

8

What is a lariat?

9

What are longhorns?

10

What was pemmican?

11

What was a prairie schooner?

12

What were the pioneers' draft animals?

WORLD HISTORY 2
THE YEAR 1492

1

Which royal couple backed Columbus?

2

Which was the last Muslim kingdom in Spain?

3

What happened to this kingdom in 1492?

4

Who were told to leave Spain in 1492?

5

What holy office did a Borgia acquire in 1492?

6

"The Magnificent", he died May 9, 1492. Who was he?

7

Pierro della Francesca died; who was he?

8

How many ships were used by Christopher Columbus in his voyage?

9

When Columbus landed, where did he think he was?

10

Where was the Kingdom of Kongo?

11

Which European country made contact with Kongo?

12

Which novel maths symbols made sums easier?

WORLD HISTORY 2
MIXED BAG

1

Where was the World's Fair at which President McKinley was shot?

2

Whose mistress was Clara Petacci?

3

What did Howard Carter and Lord Carnarvon find in 1922?

4

Which was the last nation in the Americas to abolish slavery?

5

Who was the Roman god of fire?

6

Nell Gwyn was the mistress of which English king?

7

In which century did the "Black Death" decimate Europe?

8

Who was the first man to fly solo around the world?

9

In which country was Ned Kelly a celebrated outlaw?

10

Who founded the Turkish Republic ?

11

Which Chinese dynasty came first, Ming or Qing?

12

What mail service was used during the 1870 siege of Paris?

1

Where did Maria Theresa and Josef II rule?

2

Where did Franz Joseph (1848-1916) rule?

3

Where was the Revolt of Brabant, 1789-90?

4

Where was Mazzini a nation-builder?

5

From which country did King Alfonso XIII flee in 1931?

6

Where did Margrethe II succeed King Frederick IX in 1972?

7

How many republics have there been in France?

8

Who was the "Sun King"?

9

Which country lost Alsace and Lorraine in 1871?

10

Where was Constantine deposed in 1967?

11

Where is the crown of St Stephen treasured?

12

Where was Imre Nagy forced out in 1956?

1

What was the first metal used to make tools?

2

How did the Swedes "change sides" in 1967?

3

Which "Golden State" joined the USA in 1850?

4

Who was General Tojo?

5

In what year was NATO founded?

6

Which civilization built Machu Picchu?

7

In what year was Nelson Mandela released from prison?

8

Who demanded "liberty, equality, fraternity"?

9

Who succeeded President Lincoln?

10

Where did Blackshirts march in 1922?

11

In which year did the Russian Revolution begin?

12

What was tested at Alamogordo, 16 July 1945?

1

For whom did Lou Gehrig play baseball, from 1925?

2

How many title bouts did boxer Rocky Marciano lose?

3

Who was "Papa Bear"?

4

Who beat Ken Rosewall in the 1974 Wimbledon men's final?

5

Who was the Manassa Mauler?

6

Who was stripped of a 1988 sprint gold medal for drug-taking?

7

What game did Richard Bergmann play?

8

For which country did Diego Maradona play soccer?

9

Which championship did Bobby Jones win in 1930?

10

In which year were the first US Open Tennis Championships held?

11

In which 1908 race was Pietri disqualified?

12

And why?

1

Which jungle hero was created by Edgar Rice Burroughs?

2

Who directed the original *Pyscho* movie?

3

Who wrote *The Pit and the Pendulum*?

4

Who was pursued by Van Helsing?

5

Who was the dark side of Dr Jekyll?

6

And who wrote about them?

7

Who wrote the gory play *Titus Andronicus*?

8

What did the Gorgon do to anyone who saw her?

9

Which book features Quasimodo and bells?

10

And who was its 19th-century French author?

11

Whose monster was played in 1931 by Boris Karloff?

12

What was The Blob in the 1958 horror film?

1

Where were Chaucer's pilgrims bound?

2

Which Scottish poet wrote "Auld Lang Syne"?

3

What was Fabergé famous for making?

4

What can be Persian, Indian, and Turkish?

5

Who sculpted "The Thinker"?

6

In which century did the Romantic movement begin?

7

Which Greek was "the father of history"?

8

Which 1719 book about a castaway was a bestseller?

9

What did Sheraton design?

10

Where was the original Meissen factory?

11

Who was Cervantes' most famous creation?

12

For what were Reynolds and Gainsborough famed?

CULTURE & SOCIETY
FIRST IN THEIR FIELD

. . . .

1

Which year saw the first plane fly across the English Channel?

. . . .

2

Who made the cartoon "talkie" *Steamboat Willie* (1928)?

. . . .

3

First "wild-card" team to win a Super Bowl (1981)?

. . . .

4

What year was the first London Marathon?

. . . .

5

What was Edward Whymper first on top of in 1865?

. . . .

6

Who was Arthur Ashe?

. . . .

7

Who was the first US winner of the F1 title (1961)?

. . . .

8

Dutch woman athlete who won 4 golds at the 1948 Olympics?

. . . .

9

What first did Monica Seles achieve in 1991?

. . . .

10

What first did Gertrude Ederle achieve in 1926?

. . . .

11

Which was the first Bond film?

. . . .

12

How did André-Jacques Garnerin come down in 1797?

. . . .

1

In which sport did Abebe Bikila excel?

2

Winner of the Preakness and Kentucky Derby in 1964?

3

What did Angela Mortimer win in 1961?

4

Died 1966, said by Muhammad Ali to be "the greatest"?

5

Which team won the 1966 soccer World Cup?

6

In golf, who won his second US Open in 1967?

7

And whose 1948 record score did he beat?

8

For what team did Joe Namath star in 1969?

9

Whose 1969 Wimbledon tennis match lasted 5hr 12 min?

10

And who won?

11

How did vaulter George Davies innovate in 1961?

12

Where were the 1964 summer Olympics held?

1

Who was "Baby Face" Nelson?

2

Who led the best-known Confederate guerrilla band?

3

Who was 1930s America's "Public Enemy No. 1"?

4

Who said Rome was "a city of necks... for me to chop"?

5

Which outlaw was killed by Texas Rangers in 1878?

6

Who ordered the St Valentine's Day massacre?

7

What was 1970s New York City serial killer David Berkowitz known as?

8

Who was the "Oklahoma Bomber"?

9

Which gang was led by the notorious bank robber Butch Cassidy?

10

Which murder suspect was arrested in Montreal in 1909?

11

Which crimes were attributed to Albert DeSalvo?

12

How was Ilich Ramirez Sanchez better known?

CULTURE & SOCIETY
MIXED BAG

1

What was Rudolph Valentino's cause of death?

2

In which town in Texas was Roy Orbison born?

3

Who flew on stage for the first time in 1904?

4

Which Josephine was the talk of Paris in the 1920s?

5

In which city was Charlie Chaplin born?

6

Who was Hollywood's "platinum blonde"?

7

Who was Lucy in the long-running TV show?

8

In which play does Professor Higgins appear?

9

Which hero of Greek myth had a heel weakness?

10

Whose wife was Sharon Tate, murdered in 1969?

11

What was the Beatles' own record label?

12

Lichtenstein and Johns were art exponents of what?

1

What year was Alcatraz closed?

2

In which American city was Walnut Street Jail (1790s)?

3

What criminal career did the 18th-century Anne Bonny pursue?

4

Of whom was Martha Tabram one of several victims?

5

What was a medieval "hue and cry"?

6

What was "Old Sparky," first used in 1890?

7

Which serial killer gave himself an astrological nickname?

8

What was the medieval punishment for traitors?

9

Which "man for all seasons" was beheaded, 1535?

10

What is the oldest prison in California (1852)?

11

Who did John Hinckley Jr take a shot at in 1981?

12

What was France's "national razor"?

1

Which sport event was first held at St Moritz in 1884?

2

James Naismith is said to have started what in 1891?

3

What did Louis XI of France play on a table?

4

What did Americans play after nine pins were banned (1840s)?

5

Which two Olympic champions went on to play Tarzan on film?

6

In which decade was "Blue Moon" a hit for the first time?

7

What game did Bill Tilden play?

8

Who beat Sonny Liston in 1964?

9

Who in 1920 became president of the American PFA?

10

Which movie star famously wanted to be left alone?

11

Which was arguably the most famous American racehorse?

12

Which hockey trophy dates from 1894?

1

What was Milo of Croton good at?

2

What did Olympic athletes wear in Ancient Greece?

3

Who got a wooden sword when he retired?

4

What did a confector do in the Roman arena?

5

What was a quarterstaff?

6

What was a singlestick?

7

Who practiced at the butts?

8

What was popinjay shooting?

9

Who practiced with a quintain?

10

What was tilting at the ring all about?

11

What was staged in Rome's Circus Maximus?

12

Which Greek athletes use weights for extra propulsion?

1

In which year was the first America's Cup?

2

What were first raced in Paris in 1968?

3

Which hot-air ballooning trophy is named after a US newspaper tycoon?

4

Which game's origin is Abner Doubleday linked?

5

What did the Hoboken Knickerbocker Club play?

6

Which Hollywood actress won 10 World Skating Championships?

7

Which people played Harpastum?

8

Who played a game called Tichtli?

9

What is the name of the most famous dog sled race, set in Alaska?

10

Which game may originate with the Persian "shah"?

11

In what did Eddie Arcaro and Gordon Richards star?

12

What did Matthew Webb do first in 1875?

CULTURE & SOCIETY
CRIME FICTION

1

In which precinct did Ed McBain set many stories?

2

In which 1930s thrillers did Nick and Nora Charles appear?

3

Which sleuth appeared on book jackets with a halo?

4

Who became known as the Queen of Crime?

5

Whose book *The Moving Target* features private eye Lew Harper?

6

Which French writer wrote a letter titled *J'accuse*?

7

Which hard-boiled private eye calls his gun "Betsy"?

8

Why was the author of *Tom Jones* often in court?

9

Which Irish wit wrote *Lord Arthur Savile's Crime*?

10

And in which jail did he serve two years?

11

Who lived at 221B Baker Street?

12

And who was his arch-enemy?

1

Which philosopher wrote *Leviathan*?

2

What nationality was Karl Marx?

3

Who invented psychoanalysis?

4

What nationality was Thomas Aquinas?

5

Why were Greek Stoics so named?

6

Which apostle founded the Western Christian Church?

7

Who led his followers to Medina in 622?

8

In which country was Buddha born?

9

Who taught the Way or Dao?

10

In which religion did the Ark feature?

11

Who was Guru Nanak?

12

Where did Jainism develop?

1

What was Joseph Conrad's native language?

2

Who was the Greek god of love?

3

Who wrote about a white whale?

4

How was the Greek philosopher Socrates made to take his own life?

5

In which country did Giotto and Raphael paint?

6

In which European country did Molière write his plays?

7

According to Malory, what there were 150 of?

8

Who did Ancient Egyptians think Nut was?

9

Who was considered the greatest of all Roman orators?

10

What revolutionary party did Robespierre lead?

11

By what name is Kongfuzi better known?

12

Who wrote about "utilitarianism"?

1

Which John always sang in black?

2

Which John assassinated Abraham Lincoln?

3

Which John's first major movie was *A Nightmare on Elm Street*?

4

Which John created Harry "Rabbit" Angstrom?

5

Which John was one of *The Dirty Dozen*?

6

Which John signed the Magna Carta?

7

Which John was a jazz saxophonist who died in 1967?

8

Which John is a classical guitarist?

9

Which John was a folk singer who died in a plane crash in 1997?

10

Which John won an Oscar for *Ryan's Daughter*?

11

Which John was a famous 20th-century UK economist?

12

Which John was "public enemy number one"?

1

Who was "Joltin' Joe"?

2

Who was "The Gipper"?

3

Who said "you are the pits of the world" ?

4

Who was The Wizard of Menlo Park?

5

Which golfer's nickname was "Fuzzy"?

6

Which team had the Big Blue Wrecking Crew?

7

Who was "Smoking Joe"?

8

What did Bob Beamon do in 1968?

9

Norma Jean Baker/Mortensen became... who?

10

Who was "Little Mo"?

11

Who was Althea Gibson?

12

Who was the "Flying Finn" ?

CULTURE & SOCIETY
MYTH AND MISCELLANY

1

In Greek myth, whose wings melted?

2

How many gospels are there in the New Testament?

3

How many deadly sins were there?

4

How long did Phileas Fogg's journey take?

5

Which pond plants did Claude Monet like to paint?

6

Whose poems are collected in *Leaves of Grass*?

7

Which battle of 1812 is described in *War and Peace*?

8

Which war was photographed by Matthew Brady?

9

In a Greek theater, what did actors do in the skene?

10

Who was the Greek god of the sea?

11

Whose pre-1970s currency had "tanners" and "bobs"?

12

What year did George Orwell write pessimistically about?

1

In which language was *Anna Karenina* written?

2

In which country is *Kidnapped* set?

3

Where did Impressionists first show their work?

4

Who wrote the play *Hedda Gabler*?

5

What did Diaghilev start in 1909?

6

Which Dutch artist killed himself in 1890?

7

What was the book *A Night to Remember* about?

8

Which president wrote *Profiles of Courage*?

9

Which British prime minister painted as a hobby?

10

What kind of buildings did Louis Sullivan design?

11

Which 1950s movement opposed all things "square"?

12

Who designed the Guggenheim Museum, New York?

183

CULTURE & SOCIETY
CULTURE MATTERS

1

What kind of pictures did Robert Capa take?

2

Why were Alexander Calder's creations moving?

3

How many Graces did Canova sculpt?

4

Who first danced Stravinsky's ballet *Rite of Spring*?

5

Which Roman general wrote a history of the Gallic Wars?

6

Who was Marcel Marceau?

7

Where did Antonio Gaudi mostly work?

8

What does the Venus de Milo lack?

9

Which poem begins, "Hamelin Town's in Brunswick..."?

10

In which Noel Coward play does a wifely ghost return?

11

What, according to Anita Loos, do gentlemen prefer?

12

How does Sidney Carton die in a Dickensian tale?

CULTURE & SOCIETY
OLD-TIME COUNTRY CRAFTS

1

What was husbandry?

2

What did a fowler do?

3

What did a cooper make?

4

What did a warrener look after?

5

What was winnowing?

6

What did people make in churns?

7

What was an adze?

8

What did drovers do?

9

What was a gin-trap?

10

What was gleaning?

11

What was a wainwright's job?

12

What were carters?

1

What made a 1949 US rocket historic?

2

When was the first satellite launched?

3

What was its name?

4

Which was the third nation to launch a satellite?

5

What was *Explorer*, January 31, 1958?

6

Where did *Luna 2* land, September 1959?

7

What was *Surveyor I* (1966)?

8

Where did Soviet *Venera* probes go?

9

What first did *Viking* achieve in 1976?

10

What was *Buran*?

11

What was *Mir*?

12

Where did *Sojourner's* robot crawl in 1997?

1

What were the first locks made from?

2

What was medieval glue made from?

3

What was a shaduf used for?

4

Which Greek gave his name to a lifting screw?

5

Where were the first windmills used?

6

What did Newcomen invent in 1712?

7

What decade was nylon invented?

8

What did Volta invent in 1800?

9

What were Bakelite and Perspex early forms of?

10

What did Elisha Otis invent?

11

Who first made cement that set underwater?

12

What century was wallpaper first used?

1

What was Eli Whitney's 1793 invention?

2

What did van Leeuwenhoek peer through (1600s)?

3

Which French scientist saw that bacteria caused decay?

4

How did Nicolas Appert keep food fresh (1809)?

5

Which came first: washing machines or detergents?

6

Whose safety razor made his name?

7

What did Crapper and Bramah design?

8

Where was the first big national bank?

9

How did Greeks fasten their clothing?

10

What Christmas custom began after 1843?

11

What doctor's aid did Laennec invent (1816)?

12

What did dentist Horace Wells pioneer?

1

Who used a carbolic spray to kill germs (1875)?

2

With what 1928 discovery is Fleming associated?

3

What did Oliver Evans drive in Philadelphia in 1804?

4

Where did Benz drive the first car?

5

What did John Dunlop give to cycling?

6

Who produced the Tin Lizzie?

7

What signals did Chappé invent in 1791?

8

What did Gutenberg invent?

9

What did the Biro brothers give the world?

10

What did Clarence Birdseye pioneer in the 1920s?

11

Whose model of the atom was revealed in 1911?

12

What did Lyle Goodhue spray in 1941?

. . . .

1
What lamp did Humphry Davy design?

2
What kind of machine won the 1829 Rainhill trials?

3
What was Bushnell's *Turtle* of 1776?

4
What did Felix Wankel invent (1956)?

5
In what element did an autogyro operate?

6
What did Pascal count on in 1642?

7
What was Colossus (1940s)?

8
What did Cockerell float on air?

9
Who tapped the letter S across the Atlantic in 1901?

10
What was a phonograph?

11
Which machine did Isaac Singer perfect?

12
Which 1985 "car" had a battery and pedals?

···

1

Why was *Turbinia* (1894) sensational?

···

2

Who built the 1802 steam tug *Charlotte Dundas*?

···

3

Who was Robert Fulton?

···

4

Can you name Fulton's 1807 steamboat?

···

5

And on which river it carried passengers?

···

6

What were the *Titanic*'s sister ships?

···

7

What ocean did *Savannah* cross in 1819?

···

8

What propulsion method did early steamers use?

···

9

Where did the *Enterprise* steam in 1825?

···

10

Who built the *Great Western* in 1837?

···

11

What was the historic feat of *Sirius* in 1838?

···

12

Which was more powerful: screw or paddle-wheel?

···

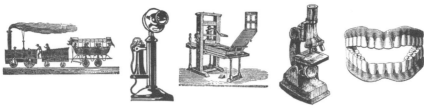

SCIENCE & LIFE
FOOD

. . . .

1

What had Henry D. Perky the idea for in 1893?'

2

What did William Brownrigg make in 1741?

3

What did Ruben Rausing invent in the 1960s?

4

What was first called "Eskimo Pie" (1927)?

5

What did John Pemberton invent in 1886?

6

What decade was instant coffee introduced?

7

Which Europeans first ate with forks?

8

In which country did burgers originate?

9

What was a trencher?

10

What is John Montagu said to have first eaten, 1762?

11

What were first licked at St Louis in 1904?

12

What were first sold in cans in 1880?

SCIENCE & LIFE
AROUND THE HOUSE

192

1

How did package-wrapping becoming easier in 1930?

2

What speeded up office letter-writing in the 1860s?

3

How did Bissell make housework easier in 1876?

4

What was Poulsen's 1898 "telegraphone"?

5

What did James Dewar invent in 1892?

6

What were snuffers used for?

7

What did John Walker strike in 1826?

8

What did Hubert Booth demonstrate in 1901?

9

In which decade did Kleenex tissues first go on sale?

10

What did Schick patent in 1931?

11

Who were the first people to use toilet paper?

12

When did toilet rolls catch on?

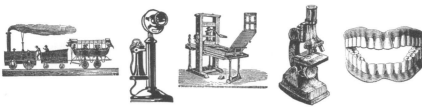

SCIENCE & LIFE
FASHION

1

Where was a periwig worn?

2

What did "gallowses" hold up?

3

What were "mutton-chops"?

4

What was a Roman strophium?

5

What began life as workwear in the 1880s?

6

What two-piece hit the fashion world in 1946?

7

How did Egyptians use lotus leaves?

8

Who gave the world "sideburns"?

9

Which people first used umbrellas?

10

When did the term "shampoo" come into use?

11

What kind of garment was a farthingale?

12

How did men in the 1700s keep their socks up?

SCIENCE & LIFE
POT LUCK

1

What was the 1951 "Ann Barton"?

2

What rolled out at Humpty Dumpty Store (1937)?

3

What did Eastman market in 1888?

4

What decade did the first Walkman appear?

5

What did Romans call "Indian salt"?

6

Who first used balance scales for weighing?

7

Which buildings had lych-gates?

8

What might have "ball and claw feet"?

9

What was a cote-hardie?

10

What instrument did Cristofori invent?

11

What did Joseph Merlin strap on (1759)?

12

What game did Charles Darrow dream up (1933)?

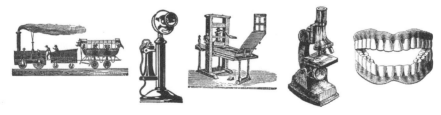

1

Who wore a chiton?

2

In which civilization did women go topless?

3

Who wore togas?

4

Who wore stolas?

5

Who dyed their skin with woad?

6

Where was a wimple worn?

7

What was the Regency pelisse?

8

What kind of garb were "Oxford bags"?

9

What were "winkle pickers"?

10

Where was a ruff worn?

11

What was a chatelaine?

12

What were Homburgs, trilbys, and stetsons?

1

What was brimstone?

2

Which Roman emperor appointed his horse a consul?

3

When were cash registers first used?

4

What was Christiaan Barnard's claim to fame?

5

What did Romans do in the lavatorium?

6

What was a gargoyle's function?

7

How did Crawford Long knock out people (1840s)?

8

Whose face is said to have launched a thousand ships?

9

What flying phenomena was sighted and given a new name in 1947?

10

Which Greek was the "Father of Medicine"?

11

In which decade were photocopiers invented?

12

What did Porsche build the first of in 1936?

SCIENCE & LIFE
INTO THE FUTURE

1

Who predicted telecoms satellites in 1946?

2

What TV data system started in 1963?

3

What were "Unimates"?

4

Who invented the first telegraph code?

5

Who first used a telephone (1876)?

6

What sort of machine is the TGV?

7

Of what was Denis Gabor a pioneer?

8

Which US spacecraft sank in 1961?

9

What decade did home video recording start?

10

What did Tim Berners-Lee help create?

11

Where were quasars spotted in 1963?

12

What did Edwin Land invent?

1

Who built the H4 *Spruce Goose*?

2

And what kind of plane was it?

3

What was the Comet's distinction?

4

Which was the fastest airliner in service?

5

What did Giffard fly in 1852?

6

Which country flew Zeppelins?

7

And which Zeppelin crashed in the US (1937)?

8

What first did the Heinkel 178 achieve?

9

Which ocean did Branson and Linstrand fly in 1991?

10

Which Renaissance artist drew a helicopter?

11

What did Robert Watson-Watt invent?

12

Which was the first big-selling jetliner?

SCIENCE & LIFE
POTPOURRI

1

What did John Smeaton build in 1759?

2

What did John Harrison make in the 1700s?

3

When were buttons first made in factories?

4

Who flew a kite in a thunderstorm in 1752?

5

Which fabric took its name from Mosul?

6

What did Bunsen invent in the 1800s?

7

What was a "turnspit"?

8

When did people first wear false teeth?

9

What pill did Pincus and others develop (1950s)?

10

What did Cousteau swim with in the 1940s?

11

Which ancient people first used cosmetics?

12

What did Macintosh and Hancock invent (1820s)?

1

Which 1872 voyage ended with a deserted ship?

2

Why were wooden ships copper-bottomed?

3

What was a clipper?

4

Who made his scientific voyages on the ship *HMS Beagle*?

5

In which ship did Francis Drake circumnavigate the world?

6

What was special about USS *Princeton*?

7

In which century did warships first have turrets?

8

Name the Greenpeace ship blown up in Auckland Harbor in 1985.

9

What was USS *Nautilus* (1955)?

10

How was *La Gloire* (1859) unusual?

11

What replaced oars for steering, from 1200?

12

What was called "a cheesebox on a raft"?

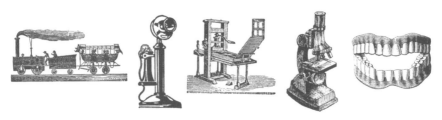

ANSWERS
PEOPLE & PLACES

. . . .

WHO WAS...?

. . . .

1. John Glenn; 2. Geronimo; 3. Edward Gibbon; 4. Isadora Duncan;
5. Marilyn Monroe; 6. Roman emperor Nero; 7. Pontius Pilate; 8. Solomon;
9. Mark Twain; 10. Marcus Tullius Cicero; 11. Myles Standish;
12. Valentina Tereshkova

WHERE?

. . . .

1. Mexico; 2. Central America (Mexico, as far south as Guatemala); 3. Poland;
4. Germany; 5. Albania; 6. Russia; 7. Britain; 8. Paris, France; 9. India;
10. China; 11. The Sistine Chapel in the Vatican, Rome; 12. Sweden

DISTINGUISHED WOMEN

. . . .

1. Ancient Egypt; 2. Woodrow Wilson; 3. Track and field as a sprinter (three
medals in the 1960 Olympics); 4. Astronomy; 5. French; 6. Jane Seymour;
7. Mother Teresa of Calcutta; 8. Calamity Jane; 9. Catherine the Great;
10. Medicine; 11. William Shakespeare;
12. The Christian Science movement

DATES

. . . .

1. Noah Webster; 2. The *Titanic*; 3. The American Declaration of
Independence; 4. September 3, 1939; 5. Jamestown, Virginia; 6. 1800;
7. Tutankhamun's; 8. It is the earliest date on which Easter can fall;
9. The president's (and vice president's); 10. India;
11. 1803; 12. The Seven Years' War

ANSWERS
PEOPLE & PLACES

....

AFRICAN AMERICANS

....

1. Stevie Wonder; 2. The Boston Massacre; 3. *Amistad*; 4. Nat Turner;
5. William Lloyd Garrison; 6 The North Star; 7. Scott was a slave who lost his
case in the US Supreme Court, having argued that residence in a free state
made him free; 8. The Underground Railroad; 9. Agriculture;
10. Booker T. Washington; 11. W.E.B. Du Bois; 12. Marcus Garvey

....

MEMORABLE WORDS

....

1. Al Jolson in the first "talkie," *The Jazz Singer*, 1927; 2. George Washington;
3. George Washington; 4. Oliver in Charles Dickens' *Oliver Twist*;
5. Bismarck, in 1863; 6. Archimedes; 7. Kodak cameras; 8. Joseph Stalin;
9. Harry S. Truman, on his desk; 10. Henry Morton Stanley, on meeting
Livingstone in 1871 in Africa; 11. Pussy-cat in the nonsense verse
The Owl and the Pussy-cat by Edward Lear; 12. Winston Churchill,
broadcasting in 1941

....

NAMES OLD AND NEW

....

1. Thailand; 2. Benin (West Africa); 3. Ghana; 4. Southern Rhodesia;
5. Belize; 6. China; 7. New York; 8. Tasmania; 9. Mumbai; 10. Basutoland;
11. Leningrad; 12. Namibia

....

AMERICAN MISCELLANY

....

1. Pulitzer Prize (first African-American winner); 2. Brooklyn Bridge;
3. William Bradford; 4. Daniel Carter Beard (1850-1941), National Scout
Commissioner; 5. The Cheyenne; 6. Bing Crosby; 7. Colin Powell (1989);
8. Henry David Thoreau; 9. Baseball—first black player in major league,
1947; 10. Little Rock, Arkansas; 11. The Black Panther Party (1966);
12. The Presidency, as an independent

....

ANSWERS
PEOPLE & PLACES

....

BIRTHS AND DEATHS

....

1. Abraham Lincoln; 2. Blenheim Palace; 3. The Olympic Games;
4. J. Edgar Hoover; 5. Allan Pinkerton; 6. Baroness Orczy; 7. Bram Stoker;
8. Dr Benjamin Spock; 9. Mario Puzo; 10. Roald Amundsen;
11. J. D. Salinger; 12. Charlotte Brontë

....

HEROES AND VILLAINS

....

1. Outlaw Jesse James; 2. Piracy; 3. Eliot Ness; 4. The Alamo;
5. He gave his life in a train crash to save his passengers, 1900;
6. Benedict Arnold; 7. She was burned at the stake; 8. Bonnie Parker and
Clyde Barrow ("Bonnie and Clyde"); 9. He committed suicide with a cyanide
capsule after being arrested; 10. An apple (according to the story);
11. Grendel; 12. John Paul Jones

....

WHO SAID IT?

....

1. George Washington; 2. Daniel Webster (1782-1852); 3. Daniel Webster;
4. The "big battalions"; 5. O. Henry; 6. Emily Dickinson;
7. Herbert Hoover; 8. Phineas T. Barnum (1810-91);
9. Benjamin Franklin; 10. John F. Kennedy, 1961; 11. Karl Marx;
12. Napoleon Bonaparte

....

POTPOURRI

....

1. India; 2. Kwame Nkrumah; 3. France; 4. A steamboat;
5. Pluto; 6. In an airship (1926). 7. American abolitionist John Brown;
8. She was beheaded at Fotheringhay Castle; 9. Sri Lanka (Mrs Sirimavo
Bandaranaike); 10. A frontiersman (1809-68);
11. The Cresta Run (tobogganing); 12. Native American tribes

....

ANSWERS
PEOPLE & PLACES

. . . .

GENERAL KNOWLEDGE

1. The soccer World Cup; 2. Boston; 3. South Africa;
4. Vienna, 1815; 5. Boston; 6. Thomas Jefferson; 7. The Civil War (1864);
8. Two of the landing beaches used during the D-Day invasion, Normandy,
1944; 9. Andrew Jackson; 10. France; 11. She was the first woman mayor in
the US (Argonia, Kansas); 12. Ayatollah Ruhollah Khomeini, leader of the
1979 Iranian revolution

WHO WERE THEY?

1. Donald Wills Douglas (1892-1981); 2. Hubert Humphrey;
3. Thomas Alva Edison (first phonograph recording); 4. W.L. Mackenzie King;
5. James Fennimore Cooper; 6. Tom Bradley (1973); 7. Melvil Dewey;
8. Hank Williams; 9. Aaron Copland; 10. Pele (Edson Arantes do Nascimento);
11. Bobby Jones; 12. Mohammed Reza Pahlavi

US HISTORIC PLACES

1. Connecticut (Guilford); 2. Georgia; 3. Rhode Island; 4. Cambridge,
Massachusetts; 5. Nebraska; 6. Indiana; 7. Oklahoma City, Oklahoma;
8. Ohio (1833); 9. Wyoming; 10. California (1812); 11. Marshall (1863-65);
12. New Jersey

BUILDINGS IN HISTORY

1. The British prime minister; 2. Seattle; 3. 17th and 18th ;
4. Washington DC; 5. 19th; 6. New York City; 7. Frank Lloyd Wright;
8. Windsor Castle; 9. Peter Stuyvesant; 10. Chicago; 11. Wyoming; 12. 1931

ANSWERS
PEOPLE & PLACES

. . . .

FAMOUS QUOTES

. . . .

1. Napoleon; 2. Winston Churchill (radio 1939); 3. Benjamin Disraeli, on
the question "Is man an ape or an angel?"; 4. 1898, after the blowing up
of USS *Maine* in Havana, Cuba; 5. Oliver Cromwell, 1653, referring to the
Speaker's mace in the English parliament; 6. Dwight D. Eisenhower;
7. John F. Kennedy; 8. Nikita Khrushchev; 9. Washington, DC, June 15, 1963;
10. Franklin D. Roosevelt; 11. General Douglas MacArthur; 12. Mao Zedong

NATIVE AMERICAN HISTORY

. . . .

1. The Black Hawk War; 2. Teotihuacan (over 200,000 inhabitants);
3. The Navajo; 4. Tanned deer hide; 5. An ice game in which players competed
to slide a spear the farthest; 6. Record-keeping and counting—a quipu was
a knotted cord; 7. Stone tools, also called fluted points (from Folsom, New
Mexico); 8. A rawhide bag or pouch; 9. The host gave gifts to guests at a
feast; 10. "Village," in Spanish; 11. A tribal leader among Eastern Woodland
Indians; 12. Sitting Bull

BADDIES AND GOODIES

. . . .

1. An ax (she was acquitted in 1893); 2. Mahatma Gandhi
(Mahatma = Great Soul); 3. Al Capone; 4. Italy; 5. William Wallace;
6. Witches; 7. Edward Teach; 8. Dashiel Hammett, *The Thin Man*; 9. Spain;
10. Oliver H. Perry; 11. Audie Murphy, later a Hollywood actor;
12. Rasputin's

FAMOUS PEOPLE

. . . .

1. Thomas Paine; 2. Charles II; 3. Richard Nixon; 4. John Paul Jones;
5. Dance; 6. Erle Stanley Gardner; 7. The Ringling Brothers; 8. Woodrow
Wilson; 9. Judy Garland; 10. George Washington; 11. Marian Anderson, after
she was banned from singing in Constitution Hall; 12. Henry Clay

ANSWERS
PEOPLE & PLACES

. . . .

FAMOUS PEOPLE NAMED P...

. . . .

1. Paganini; 2. Dorothy Parker; 3. George S. Patton; 4. Plato; 5. Pizarro;
6. Pocahontas; 7. George Mortimer Pullman; 8. Elvis Presley; 9. Juan Peron;
10. Joseph Pulitzer (1847-1911); 11. Pablo Picasso; 12. Pericles

. . . .

POTPOURRI

. . . .

1. Herbert Hoover; 2. Michael Dukakis; 3. Stan Laurel;
4. Frances Folsom Cleveland (21 in 1886); 5. Bill Clinton;
6. Abraham Lincoln; 7. Boston; 8. Captain James Cook of England;
9. Anchorage; 10. London Bridge; 11. The Cheyenne;
12. University of Mississippi

. . . .

AMERICAN COLONIAL LIFE

. . . .

1. How to plant corn; 2. Manhattan Island; 3. King Philip;
4. Indentured servants, who had to raise their voyage-fare after arrival in
America; 5. The colony's first African slaves; 6. The first elected law-making
assembly (1619); 7. A child's bed, stored beneath an adult's mattress-bed;
8. Saugus, Massachusetts; 9. Boston and New York; 10. Boston, 1690;
11. Witchcraft; 12. Sunday observance

. . . .

SOME MORE FAMOUS AMERICANS

. . . .

1. Frank Capra; 2. Jack Johnson; 3. Douglas MacArthur; 4. James Monroe;
5. Gwyneth Paltrow; 6. William L. Shirer; 7. Zachary Taylor;
8. Martha Graham; 9. General Sherman; 10. Jackie Robinson;
11. Dean Acheson; 12. Milton Berle

. . . .

ANSWERS
PEOPLE & PLACES

. . . .

COUPLES

. . . .

1. Alexandra; 2. Napoleon; 3. Prince Albert; 4. Cleopatra; 5. Romeo;
6. President Eisenhower; 7. Oranges; 8. The Prince of Wales, briefly
Edward VIII, later Duke of Windsor; 9. Lucille Ball;
10. Robert Browning; 11. John F. Kennedy; 12. Fred Astaire

. . . .

AN AMERICAN MISCELLANY

. . . .

1. Johnny Cash; 2. The Alamo; 3. Marshall; 4. Tennis; 5. Dayton, Tennessee;
6. New York City; 7. She was the first English child born in America, 1587;
8. The Library of Congress; 9. Detroit; 10. Formula One Grand Prix motor
racing drivers' championship; 11. Ulysses; 12. Patty Hearst

. . . .

MORE PEOPLE AND PLACES

. . . .

1. Colorado; 2. A composer, of symphonies and experimental music.
3. Mexican cowboys; 4. Puerto Rico, in 1493 on his 2nd voyage;
5. The White House; 6. West Virginia; 7. E.B. White; 8. Sierra Nevada;
9. A migrant party became snowbound and survivors ate the dead; 10. Credit
unions; 11. Quebec; 12. The US Naval Academy at Annapolis, Maryland

. . . .

CITY HISTORY

. . . .

1. Cincinatti; 2. Boston (The Latin School, 1635); 3. Salt Lake City;
4. Philadelphia, in the 1750s; 5. Portsmouth, New Hampshire;
6. New Orleans; 7. New York (now Columbia University);
8. The discovery of gold nearby; 9. Montreal, Canada; 10. Boston;
11. Miami; 12. "Cowtown"

. . . .

ANSWERS
WORLD HISTORY 1

. . . .

ANCIENT (1)

. . . .

1. Extinct dinosaurs; 2. A human skull found in southern England in 1912 turned out to be a fake; 3. Pre-Ice Age humans; 4. Neanderthals; 5. New Stone Age; 6. It became an island; 7. Mammoths; 8. A giant wild ox; 9. Tilled the soil, it was a primitive plough; 10. Flint; 11. On the Italy-Austria border—the remains were those of a 5000-year-old Alpine traveler; 12. Stonehenge

ANCIENT (2)

. . . .

1. Karnak, Egypt; 2. The Minoans; 3. Egypt; 4. Israelites left Egypt, led by Moses; 5. Shipbuilding and sea trading; 6. Babylon; 7. China; 8. It was the first date in their calendar; 9. Egypt; 10. Babylon; 11. The Indus; 12. Africa

WORLD WAR I

. . . .

1. Archduke Franz Ferdinand and wife Sophie; 2. Cousin; 3. 3. Belgium;
4. 1914; 5. A sword made them conspicuous to snipers; 6. Ambulance driver;
7. Real name Margarethe Zelle, she was shot as a spy;
8. The British royal family (from Saxe-Coburg-Gotha); 9. The *Lusitania*;
10. President Woodrow Wilson; 11. November 11, 1918; 12. Germany

VICE PRESIDENTS

. . . .

1. Aaron Burr and George Clinton; 2. Both resigned as vice president;
3. George Bush; 4. Coolidge and Ford; 5. The Senate; 6. Bush, while acting president during Reagan's surgery; 7. Gerald Ford in 1974, succeeding Nixon;
8. Theodore Roosevelt (42); 9. Harry S. Truman; 10. Hubert Humphrey;
11. Al Gore; 12. Richard Nixon

ANSWERS
WORLD HISTORY 1

WHICH CENTURY WAS...?

1. 18th; 2. 18th; 3. 19th; 4. 15th; 5. 11th; 6. 15th; 7. 16th; 8. 17th; 9. 18th;
10. 20th; 11. 19th; 12. 19th

HISTORICAL HORRORS

1. Vlad the Impaler; 2. Connecticut, in New England; 3. Paris in 1572;
4. He was beheaded by the Spanish; 5. Earthquake and flooding;
6. At the Bastille in Paris, he was the governor; 7. An earthquake;
8. Mongols; 9. World War II (1941); 10. Guernica; 11. Geneva, on the orders of
John Calvin; 12. The 1890 killing of 300 or so Lakota Sioux by the US Army
in South Dakota

BRITISH ROYAL TRIVIA

1. The Duke of Windsor; 2. Prince William; 3. Princess Elizabeth and Philip,
now Queen Elizabeth II and the Duke of Edinburgh; 4. Victoria;
5. The Prince of Wales and Lady Diana Spencer; 6. Diana, Princess of Wales;
7. George III; 8. James VI of Scotland, to become James I of Great Britain;
9. George V; 10. Henry VIII; 11. Princess Margaret; 12. George I

FAMOUS PARENTS & CHILDREN

1. Henry IV; 2. President Jimmy Carter; 3. Mary of Guise; 4. The Lindberghs'
son, Charles Augustus Jr.; 5. The Princess Royal, Princess Anne;
6. Prince Andrew, Duke of York and Sarah Ferguson;
7. President John F. Kennedy; 8. Abraham Lincoln; 9. John F. Kennedy;
10. Louis XIII and Anne of Austria; 11. Charlemagne; 12. Thomas Jefferson

ANSWERS

. . . .

MIDDLE AGES

. . . .

1. Harun al-Raschid's at Baghdad; 2. Charles the Great; 3. Aachen; 4. Tours;
5. He had a red beard; 6. Jerusalem; 7. Tamerlane (Tamburlaine);
8. He was wounded in the leg and was called "Timur the Lame"; 9. St Francis;
10. Cambodia; 11. A water-filled ditch around a medieval castle; 12. Monks

. . . .

RENAISSANCE EUROPE

. . . .

1. Lodovico Sforza, Duke of Milan (1451-1508); 2. The Roman Catholic
Church; 3. Geneva; 4. Aragon; 5. Leonardo Da Vinci; 6. Lorenzo Medici—"the
Magnificent"; 7. Roman Catholic bishops (at Trentino, Italy);
8. Suleiman I "the Magnificent" of Turkey; 9. Killed his own sons, so her son
could succeed him; 10. Italy; 11. Henri IV; 12. A Protestant, he became a
Roman Catholic to win over his people

. . . .

GREEKS AND GREEK MYTHS

. . . .

1. The Greek gods; 2. A stringed instrument, like a small harp;
3. Greek foot-soldiers; 4. Zeus; 5. Nine; 6. The Minotaur; 7. Crete; 8. Athens
and Sparta; 9. Foreigners; 10. Athena; 11. Shrines where people went to know
the future or the truth; 12. The Parthenon, in Athens

. . . .

ROMANS AT WAR

. . . .

1. The Etruscans; 2. One form of Roman armor; 3. Sponges on sticks;
4. Britain (AD 43); 5. A Roman artillery weapon that fired giant arrows;
6. As cavalry; 7. Stones; 8. 500; 9. A Roman legion's standard; 10. A stick;
11. A Roman cavalry soldier of the 300s onward, who wore heavy armor;
12. A curved rectangle

. . . .

ANSWERS

. . . .

1600s-1700s

41

. . . .

1. René Descartes (1596-1650); 2. Lafayette; 3. Asia (India); 4. 1781;
5. The Ming dynasty; 6. Oliver Cromwell's; 7. Lord Protector; 8. German (she
was born in Germany); 9. 6 months—he was then deposed and Catherine
took over; 10. Austrian; 11. Louis XVI of France; 12. She went to the
guillotine in 1793

. . . .

ANCIENT CIVILIZATIONS

42

. . . .

1. Iraq; 2. Sumerians; 3. An ancient writing, wedge-shaped symbols; 4. Moses;
5. Egypt; 6. Assyrian's; 7. Babylon; 8. Nebuchadnezzar of Babylon;
9. The sides form giant steps, later pyramids were smooth-sided;
10. Egypts; 11. Akhenaten of Egypt; 12. Japan

. . . .

ANCIENT TIMES

43

. . . .

1. China; 2. West Africa (Nigeria); 3. Athens, Greece; 4. Aristotle;
5. Armenian; 6. The Romans; 7. Julius Caesar and Mark Anthony;
8. The Scythians; 9. The Balkans; 10. The Celts'; 11. Attila the Hun;
12. He was murdered, by Attila, who then became sole ruler

. . . .

WORLD LEADERS

44

. . . .

1. Jawarharlal Nehru's; 2. Hitler; 3. Ariel Sharon; 4. Mohammed Ali Jinnah;
5. Scotland; 6. France; 7. 44th; 8. Peter the Great; 9. Justinian;
10. Woodrow Wilson; 11. Ronald Reagan; 12. Wilson

. . . .

ANSWERS

WORLD HISTORY 1

- -

1600-1620

- -

1. Virginia, North America; 2. Elizabeth I; 3. Russia; 4. Pocahontas;
5. Music; 6. Parliament; 7. France; 8. Hudson Bay; 9. Virginia; 10. Galileo;
11. The *Mayflower*; 12. France

- -

EVENTS IN MAY

- -

1. England, Scotland, Wales; 2. Machiavelli; 3. Adolf Hitler;
4. The *Hindenburg*; 5. The Empire State Building; 6. A US spy plane;
7. Julia Ward Howe; 8. Charles Lindbergh; 9. Brooklyn Bridge;
10. 1918 (May 15); 11. Harry S. Truman; 12. George V

- -

INDIA/PAKISTAN

- -

1. The Taj Mahal; 2. Indian National Congress; 3. Gandhi; 4. China;
5. Kashmir; 6. Goa; 7. East Pakistan (later Bangladesh); 8. Rajiv Gandhi;
9. Rajiv Gandhi; 10. Zulfikar Ali Bhutto;
11. Benazir Bhutto; 12. Bhutto, Zulfikar Ali, and Benazir

- -

20TH CENTURY

- -

1. World War I; 2. 1920s (1925); 3. An evangelist; 4. Franklin D. Roosevelt;
5. Shanty towns of unemployed families, the name was a reference to
President Hoover; 6. A drought-hit area across the Great Plains and the
southwest during the Depression; 7. President Franklin D. Roosevelt;
8. Arkansas; 9. The president sent troops to escort black students into an
all-white school; 10. Alaska and Hawaii; 11. Alan B. Shepard, Jr;
12. Washington, DC

- -

ANSWERS
POLITICS & POWER

. . . .

RULING DYNASTIES

. . . .

1. France; 2. Germany; 3. Austria; 4. Russia; 5. France and Spain; 6. Japan;
7. Indira Gandhi; 8. Japan; 9. Edward Kennedy; 10. England;
11. 1917, the year of the Russian revolution; 12. China

. . . .

THE NAME'S THE SAME

. . . .

1. Truman; 2. Ford; 3. Arthur; 4. Monroe; 5. Peter; 6. Hart – Gary, Moss and
William S.; 7. Hoover; 8. Gandhi; 9. Rogers (Robert and Ginger); 10. North;
11. McCarthy (Joseph R. and Mary); 12. Wilson

. . . .

AMERICAN PRESIDENTS

. . . .

1. Ronald Reagan; 2. Lyndon B. Johnson; 3. Woodrow Wilson;
4. First Roman Catholic, youngest elected president, at 43;
5. Ronald Reagan, 73; 6. The first, George Washington; 7. Bill Clinton;
8. Republican; 9. Herbert Hoover; 10. Lawyer; 11. Ulysses S. Grant;
12. James Buchanan

. . . .

PRESIDENTS AND PRIME MINISTERS

. . . .

1. John Adams; 2. 1940; 3. President Martin Van Buren;
4. John Major; 5. France; 6. 10 Downing Street; 7. Ronald Reagan, 1981;
8. US President Theodore Roosevelt; 9. Benazir Bhutto; 10. Canada;
11. Australia; 12. Two—John Adams and John Quincy Adams,
George Bush Sr and George W. Bush

. . . .

ANSWERS
POLITICS & POWER

· ·

THE RUSSIAN REVOLUTION

· ·

1. October 1917; 2. Lenin; 3. Czar Nicholas II; 4. The czar and his wife and children; 5. In 1918 the old Russian calendar was replaced; 6. Petrograd; 7. A moderate, he became premier in July 1917; 8. Russia's participation in World War I against Germany; 9. Moscow; 10. The Red Army; 11. The two sides in the civil war that followed the revolution; 12. *Ten Days that Shook the World*

· ·

POLITICAL WHO'S WHO?

· ·

1. Pierre Trudeau; 2. Mikhail Gorbachev; 3. Kofi Annan; 4. Joe Biden; 5. Gates; 6. Willy Brandt; 7. Dmitry Medvedev; 8. Sarah Palin; 9. Schwarzenegger; 10. Nicolas Sarkozy; 11. Dan Quayle; 12. Boris Yeltsin

· ·

POLITICAL LOSERS

· ·

1. Richard Nixon; 2. Lenin and the Bolsheviks; 3. Al Gore; 4. Senator Stephen A. Douglas; 5. Barack Obama; 6. The Conservative party; 7. Marie Antoinette; 8. Neville Chamberlain; 9. Wendell Wilkie; 10. Bill Clinton; 11. Dwight D. Eisenhower; 12. Richard Nixon

· ·

EMPIRES AND COLONIES

· ·

1. The Dutch (Dutch East Indies); 2. Cambodia, Laos and Vietnam; 3. France; 4. China; 5. Hawaii; 6. The lion; 7. The Persian Empire; 8. The Mauryan Empire, India (200s BC); 9. Egypt; 10. Nigeria; 11. Africa; 12. Ethiopia

· ·

    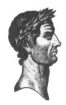

BALLOT BOX

ANSWERS
POLITICS & POWER

....

POLITICAL FIRSTS

....

1. Toussaint l'Ouverture; 2. Margaret Thatcher; 3. Theodore Roosevelt;
4. Woodrow Wilson; 5. John Adams; 6. Richard Nixon; 7. Helmut Kohl;
8. Lyndon Johnson, 1963; 9. Lexington; 10. Mary Robinson;
11. Hattie Wyatt Caraway (1932); 12. 1920

....

POT LUCK (1)

....

1. Delano; 2 Netherlands; 3 Italy; 4. Belgium; 5. Louis Philippe;
6. Irish Republican Army; 7. Napoleon Bonaparte; 8. 1979; 9. Nicholas II;
10. Two (Anne Boleyn and Katherine Howard); 11. Spain, General Franco
(1936-75); 12. Argentina

....

AROUND THE WORLD

....

1. Trostky; 2. Canada; 3. Alexander Dubcek; 4. Egypt (the Suez Canal);
5. Konrad Adenauer; 6. Ivan the Terrible (1533-84); 7. Turkey; 8. Jawaharlal
Nehru; 9. Poland; 10. Romania; 11. Gabon; 12. Bulganin and Khrushchev,
Soviet leaders

....

FAMOUS WOMEN

....

1. Elizabeth I; 2. British Prime Minister Margaret Thatcher; 3. Half-sister;
4. The Romans; 5. King George VI of Great Britain;
6. Claudia Alta Taylor, wife of Lyndon B. Johnson; 7. Calcutta; 8. Sally Ride;
9. Lucretia Mott and Elizabeth Cady Stanton; 10. King Henry II of England;
11. Adolf Hitler; 12. Marie Antoinette, who went to the guillotine in 1793

....

ANSWERS
POLITICS & POWER

. . . .

US POLITICAL FIGURES

. . . .

1. James K. Polk; 2. Samuel Gompers; 3. John Quincy Adams;
4. Andrew Jackson; 5. Thomas Jefferson; 6. Carol Moseley-Braun, in 1921;
7. Chicago; 8. 1989; 9. Theodore Roosevelt; 10. Secretary of State;
11. Bob Dole and Jack Kemp; 12. First African American woman to serve in
the US Congress (1969-83)

. . . .

FAMOUS IN THEIR DAY

. . . .

1. The Philippines; 2. Roman emperor Claudius; 3. James A. Garfield in 1881;
4. Indonesia; 5. Israel; 6. Hirohito; 7. Supreme Court judge;
8. President Taft; 9. Elizabeth I (the year was 1564); 10. Leader of Sinn Fein
in Ireland, killed 1922; 11. Prime Minister of Canada 1894-96;
12. South Africa (1984-89)

. . . .

NATIONAL LEADERS

. . . .

1. Sir Winston Churchill; 2. Prussia; 3. Mexico; 4. Colonel Qaddafi;
5. Josef Stalin; 6. Hungary; 7. General Cardenas; 8. Simon Bolivar;
9. Tanzania; 10. Canada; 11. Chile, during that country's war of
independence from Spain, 1818; 12. Sweden

. . . .

DICTATORS AND DESPOTS

. . . .

1. Haiti; 2. Romania; 3. Portugal; 4. Cambodia; 5. Uganda;
6. Benito Mussolini; 7. Saddam Hussein; 8. North Korea; 9. Stalin's;
10. Albania; 11. Bokassa (Central African Republic, 1976); 12. Zimbabwe

. . . .

ANSWERS
POLITICS & POWER

PLACES OF POWER

1. 1901; 2. Pierre L'Enfant; 3. The president of the French Republic;
4. The pope; 5. In Moscow, Russia; 6. Beijing, China;
7. The Central Intelligence Agency (CIA); 8. New York; 9. Brussels and
Strasbourg; 10. London (England); 11. Ottawa; 12. Canberra

SCANDALS

1. Edward Kennedy; 2. Monica Lewinsky, with whom President Clinton
denied he had had sex; 3. France; 4. France again, the Panama Canal Co.
collapsed; 5. Vice President of the United States; 6. *All the President's Men*;
7. New York City—a corrupt political "machine"—1800s; 8. Weapons of mass
destruction; 9. Washington, DC; 10. Bob Woodward and Carl Bernstein;
11. Joseph McCarthy 12. Oil reserves, and bribes

POT LUCK (2)

1. Sir Richard Burton; 2. Germany, in the 1920s; 3. Calvin;
4. First woman vice-presidential candidate for a US party, Democrats 1984;
5. A naval mutiny (1921) in Russia; 6. Sir Richard Burton;
7. Papa Doc; 8. Yale; 9. George Washington; 10. Egypt; 11. Paderewski;
12. Golf

ASSASSINATIONS

1. Julius Caesar; 2. Japan in the 1930s; 3. John Wilkes Booth;
4. Robert Kennedy; 5. Martin Luther King; 6. Rasputin; 7. Anwar al-Sadat;
8. The Red Brigade; 9. By a Nihilist bomb; 10. Mahatma Gandhi;
11. Lord Mountbatten; 12. John Lennon

ANSWERS
WARS & WARFARE

··

WAR AT SEA

··

1. To crash into enemy ships; 2. A 1500s/1600s warship with oars and sails;
3. The Vikings; 4. Castles were raised sections of deck fore and aft, for
soldiers; 5. World War II; 6. Lord Howard of Effingham; 7. *Bonhomme
Richard*; 8. Britain v. France and Spain; 9. HMS *Dreadnought*;
10. *Graf Spee*; 11. Japan; 12. A submarine-launched strategic missile

··

THE ALLIES AT WAR

··

1. The Allied invasion of southern France, August 1944;
2, A German submarine (U-boat); 3. The Allied landings in North Africa 1942;
4. Winston Churchill; 5. Aircraft carrier; 6. The Mustang fighter and fighter-
bomber; 7. The Solomons; 8. China/IndoChina; 9. Shoot it; BAR is Browning
Automatic Rifle; 10. Tiger; 11. The Battle of the Bulge;
12. Admiral William Frederick Halsey, Jr.

··

INVASIONS

··

1. Spain; 2. Afghanistan; 3. Suleiman the Magnificent, ruler of the Turkish
Ottomans ; 4. The Allies' invasion of Normandy, 1944; 5. 2003;
6. Russia; 7. The Armada (a great fleet); 8. Hitler's plan to invade Britain in
1940; 9. The Vikings; 10. Japan; 11. Austria-Hungary; 12. Grenada

··

MILITARY MISCELLANY (1)

··

1. The Spitfire; 2. Hitler's invasion of the USSR, 1941; 3. Glenn Miller;
4. Battleships (US and British respectively); 5. Dummy paratroopers dropped
over Normandy 1944 to confuse the Germans; 6. A US Navy fighter ace, with
34 victories; 7. American volunteers joining the RAF at the start of World
War II; 8. A German battleship, sunk in Norway in 1944;
9. Paul W. Tibbets Jr.; 10. Air raid precautions; 11. Yugoslavia;
12. Pearl Harbor

··

ANSWERS
WARS & WARFARE

. . . .

COMMANDERS

. . . .

1. Omar; 2. Artillery; 3. General Dwight D. Eisenhower; 4. El Cid;
5. Hermann Goering; 6. George S. Patton; 7. H. Norman Schwarzkopf, US
commander in the Gulf War, 1991; 8. General Sir Douglas Haig;
9. Commander of Viet Minh forces, Vietnam, 1950s; 10. Rommel;
11. Napoleon Bonaparte; all three were Marshalls in the French army;
12. Robert E. Lee

FORTS AND CASTLES

. . . .

1. Fort Dearborn; 2. It had several walls, constructed in rings;
3. The Moors; 4. An iron castle gate, which could be lowered and raised;
5. Japan (daimyos were feudal warlords); 6. The Incas; 7. India; 8. Louis XIV,
in the 17th century; 9. The attacking army surrounded a castle, trying to
starve out the defenders or breach the walls; 10. Baskets filled with soil, used
as movable shields; 11. They dug tunnels or saps, to "undermine" the walls;
12. George Washington

20TH-CENTURY WARS

. . . .

1. The Korean War; 2. Vietnam, 1954; 3. Nicaragua; 4. Iran and Iraq;
5. The Six Day War; 6. Pakistan, where East Pakistan broke away to become
Bangladesh; 7. Italy; 8. Kuwait; 9. Vietnam, 1968; 10. The Vietcong;
11. The Yom Kippur War; 12. Argentina occupied the Falklands Islands
(Malvinas), a British territory

LOSERS

. . . .

1. The Romans, to the Visigoths; 2. Chickamauga; 3. The Persians';
4. The Japanese; 5. Prussia; 6. The French; 7. Russia's; 8. The French;
9. The English; 10. The Marquis de Montcalm; 11. The 7th Cavalry;
12. The British

ANSWERS
WARS & WARFARE

. . . .

WINNERS

. . . .

1. United States; 2. Napoleon; 3. Peter the Great/Russia; 4. The battle of Waterloo, 1815; 5. Octavian (later Augustus); 6. Simon Bolivar (1783-1830), who fought the Spanish in South America; 7. Genghis Khan (1167-1227); 8. Alexander the Great; 9. William Henry Harrison; 10. Arthur Wellesley, Duke of Wellington; 11. Colonel James H. Doolittle; 12. Admiral Chester W. Nimitz

GENERALS

. . . .

1. Wellington; 2. Burgoyne; 3. Cornwallis; 4. Napoleon; 5. Chancellorsville; 6. Bradley; 7. The Red Army; 8. Stilwell; 9. Confederate cavalry raids into enemy territory; 10. Afghanistan; 11. World War I; 12. Douglas MacArthur

WEAPONS

. . . .

1. An early "machine gun"; 2. It had up to 10 barrels, cranked by a handle for rapid fire; 3. A rifle, long used by the British Army; 4. Long spear-like lances—lancers were cavalrymen; 5. Cavalry soldiers, especially in the 19th-century—it was a slashing sword; 6. A curved sword, common in Asia; 7. A type of early cannon; 8. He threw it, it was a javelin or throwing spear; 9. A longbow; 10. Very long spear-like weapons with ax heads, carried by infantry; 11. They had to ignite a charge of gunpowder, in order to fire the weapon; 12. The bayonet

MORE WEAPONRY

. . . .

1. A helmet worn by a 17th-century soldier; 2. On his lower legs; 3. His lance; 4. A cloth garment worn over armor; 5. The crossbow; 6. A sword; 7. A tubelike antitank weapon used by the US Army; 8. A musket, 18th century; 9. From the muzzle: breech-loaders were a 19th-century innovation; 10. His arrows; 11. An ancient and mysterious flame-throwing weapon; 12. Hurling stones and other missiles; it was an ancient siege engine

ANSWERS
WARS & WARFARE

· ·

ON THE MARCH

· ·

1. Gettysburg; 2. Waterloo; 3. Roman soldiers; 4. To clean inside the barrel of a rifle; 5. A Duplex-Drive amphibious truck; 6. A Landing Craft Tank (designed to land tanks); 7. To pierce plate armor—it had a hammer head and a spike; 8. 1600s to 1700s; 9. A solid mass of warriors in ranks with spears and shields; 10. Two; 11. On his helmet; 12. The lower arm

WAR AROUND THE WORLD

· ·

1. Japan; 2. Copper (later bronze); 3. Elephants; 4. Greek oared ships, with three banks of oars; 5. France and England; 6. Germany; 7. From the battlefield of Marathon to Athens, with news of the Greek victory; 8. The first really seaworthy submarine; 9. Italian patriot Garibaldi; 10. The Battle of the Little Bighorn; 11. Round; 12. Chain mail

WORLD WAR I (1)

· ·

1. 1914; 2. The tank; 3. Jutland, 1916; 4. The Turks; 5. German airships; 6. A machine gun; 7. Fighter planes; 8. Vimy Ridge, in France, where over 11,000 Canadians lost their lives during the battle of Arras, 1917; 9. American Expeditionary Force (World War I); 10. Bundles of wood carried by tanks, they were used to bridge trenches; 11. Armed merchant ships, disguised to look harmless; 12. Manfred Von Richthofen, German air ace

WORLD WAR I (2)

· ·

1. US General John Joseph Pershing, commander of US expeditionary force; 2. Second battle of Ypres; 3. Sarajevo; 4. During the retreat from Mons, 1914; 5. Seaplanes—it was the first ship built specifically for carrying aircraft; 6. Veterans Day; 7. Australian and New Zealand Army Corps; 8. Verdun; 9. A number of very large explosive mines; 10. It was the space between the opposing trenches; 11. A chemical weapon, another name for carbonyl chloride gas, first used by the Germans in 1915; 12. In East Africa, where he was a German commander, never seriously defeated

ANSWERS
WARS & WARFARE

. . . .

WORLD WAR II (1)

. . . .

1. US tanks; 2. A home-made incendiary bomb, basically a bottle filled with petrol; 3. The German Ju-87 dive-bomber; 4. An artillery weapon, one of the most effective antitank guns; 5. US Navy aircraft carriers; 6. US naval fighter planes; 7. None; it was a pilotless flying bomb; 8. Midget submarines; 9. USS *Missouri*; 10. Standard infantry carbine; 11. His helmet; 12. US heavy bombers

. . . .

WORLD WAR II (2)

. . . .

1. France, the southern half not occupied by the Nazis; 2. Protection Squadron; 3. France; 4. Chester W. Nimitz; 5. Strips of metal foil dropped by Allied bombers to confuse German radar; 6. Malta; 7. The Philippines; 8. Coding and de-coding signals, by the Germans; 9. Women in the US and Royal Navies; 10. Air Force—Commander US Strategic Air Forces, Europe, from 1944; 11. Tooey; 12. Stalingrad

. . . .

THE CIVIL WAR

. . . .

1. John Brown (anti-slavery campaigner and abolitionist); 2. Fort Sumter; 3. The Confederacy; 4. Soldiers dressed in Oriental-style uniforms; 5. The Union army; 6. Union general William T. Sherman; 7. Gettysburg; 8. Grey; 9. Grant; 10. The Battle of Nashville, one of the biggest Union victories; 11. A Confederate POW camp in Georgia; 12. He was tried and executed for war crimes, after investigation of prisoner abuse at Andersonville

. . . .

ANCIENT BATTLES

. . . .

1. Achilles; 2. King Saul; 3. Thermopylae; 4. Leonidas; 5. Philip (father of Alexander); 6. Alexander the Great; 7. Their army was beaten by Hannibal; 8. Roman slaves; 9. Spartacus; 10. Julius Caesar, who beat Pompey; 11. Brutus and Cassius, leaders of the conspiracy against Julius Caesar; 12. The second triumvirate—Octavian, Mark Antony, and Marcus Lepidus

. . . .

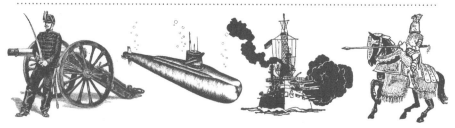

ANSWERS
WARS & WARFARE

. . . .

OLD TIME WARS

. . . .

1. Elephants; 2. Napoleon Bonaparte and Wellington; 3. 1571; 4. At sea (in the Mediterranean); 5. India; 6. 17th (1675-76); 7. Leipzig; 8. World War I; 9. Italy; 10. The Ottawa and other Native American tribes in the Middle West; 11. Europe; 12. Russian leader Alexander Nevski

. . . .

WORLD WAR I (3)

. . . .

1. Gallipoli; 2. Italy; 3. Gothas; 4. The passenger liner was torpedoed by a German submarine; 5. Great Britain; 6. Russia; 7. Jerusalem; 8. *Fires Burning*; 9. T. E. Lawrence (Lawrence of Arabia); 10. The Ottoman Turkish empire; 11. A railroad car; 12. The American Expeditionary Force (1917)

. . . .

WHO WON?

. . . .

1. Italy; 2. France; 3. Normans; 4. Russia; 5. USA; 6. The House of Lancaster; 7. Britain; 8. Rome; 9. Britain; 10. The American colonies; 11. Japan; 12. The Vietnamese (pushing out the French)

. . . .

WORLD WAR II (3)

. . . .

1. A British battleship, sunk by the Japanese; 2. United States; 3. Yamamoto; 4. His aircraft was shot down by US planes; 5. A German fighter-bomber, it was the first jet plane into combat; 6. "Lightning war"; 7. Japan's latest fighter plane; 8. Pilots of the American Volunteer Group fighting alongside the Chinese against Japan; 9. The Allied plan to para-drop troops around Arnhem and Nijmegen (Holland) and seize Rhine crossings; 10. Rosie (Rosie the Riveter became a familiar sight on posters); 11. Mussolini of Italy; 12. German tanks

. . . .

ANSWERS

WARS & WARFARE

· ·

SECRET WAR

· ·

1. It was a top-secret German facility for V-2 rockets; 2. US Civil War;
3. Office for Strategic Services (World War II)—it was the counterpart of
the British SOE and the predecessor of the CIA; 4. Coding messages, by the
Germans; 5. Japan (executed 1944); 6. Message-carrying; 7. A spy for Germany
during World War II, real name Elysa Bazna; 8. Joseph Goebbels; 9. Dutch;
10. Julius and Ethel Rosenberg were executed as spies in 1953, for giving US
atomic bomb secrets to the Russians; 11. Napoleon; 12. Napoleon

· ·

INDIAN WARS

· ·

1. 17th (1675-76); 2. A Native American chief (son of Masosoit, chief of the
Wampanoag); 3. The French and Indian Wars; 4. Pontiac's War;
5. The Shawnee; 6. Tecumseh's brother; 7. William Henry Harrison; 8. Florida;
9. The Sioux; 10. The Nez Perce; 11. Geronimo; 12. Sitting Bull

· ·

MILITARY MISCELLANY (2)

· ·

1. The US Civil War; 2. A US war correspondent, reported on the 1898
Spanish-American War; 3. Edward R. Murrow; 4. They were all World War II
fighter "aces"; 5. World War II; 6. The Vietnam War; 7. The Gulf War;
8. Adolf Eichmann; 9. He was tried for war crimes in Israel and executed;
10. The My Lai Massacre in Vietnam; 11. Nuremberg, Germany;
12. George W. Bush

· ·

POT LUCK

· ·

1. Afghanistan; 2. *Canberra* (used as a troop ship); 3. A V/STOL jump jet;
4. Iwo Jima; 5. Korean War; 6. Guantanamo Bay;
7. Russia; 8. Balkans/Kosovo; 9. US Secretary of War; 10. A chemical defoliant
used during the Vietnam War; 11. The Geneva Conventions;
12. Western Europe, they were the German defenses against Allied invasion
during World War II

ANSWERS
MODERN TIMES

....

THE YEAR 2000
....

1. The fear that "Y2K" would create many computer-related problems;
2. Zeljko Raznatovic, Serb nationalist, who used the name Arkan, was shot dead in Belgrade; 3. Venezuela; 4. Kurds', especially those in Turkey;
5. A NASA spacecraft—Eros is an asteroid; 6. The women's world figure-skating championship; 7. The New York Yankees;
8. Bill Clinton; 9. Syria; 10. Afghanistan, the Taliban cracked down on opium-production; 11. East Timor; 12. Jean Chrétien

....

MODERN MISCELLANY
....

1. A comet, named *Shoemaker-Levy-9*; 2. Hillary Clinton, in 2000;
3. US ambassador to the United Nations; 4. US economist, who replaced Alan Greenspan as chairman of the Fed (US Federal Reserve Board);
5. Alan Bennett; 6. Arnold Schwarzenegger; 7. Pierce Brosnan; 8. July 7;
9. London was named as host city for the 2012 Olympics; 10. Turkey;
11. A baby polar bear in Berlin Zoo; 12. Gordon Brown, 2007

....

PEOPLE/COUNTRY ASSOCIATIONS
....

1. Myanmar (Burma); 2. United States; 3. Nigeria; 4. Indonesia; 5. Georgia;
6. Australia; 7. Bosnia; 8. China; 9. The Philippines; 10. Malawi;
11. Denmark; 12. Iran

....

NEWSMAKERS
....

1. Scooter; 2. AOL; 3. Syria (1971-2000); 4. American actor (1920-2000);
5. Pierre Trudeau; 6. Eminem; 7. Kenya; 8. Mortgages;
9. US Treasury Secretary; 10. London, he was a former KGB agent;
11. Daniel Day-Lewis, in the film *There Will Be Blood*; 12. Gerald R. Ford

....

ANSWERS
MODERN TIMES

. . . .

THE YEAR WAS 1990

. . . .

1. General Noriega; 2. Liberia; 3. China; 4. Lithuania; 5. Mikhail Gorbachev;
6. Azerbaijan; 7. Todor Zhivkov; 8. F.W. de Klerk; 9. Nelson Mandela;
10. Czechoslovakia; 11. Nicaragua; 12. The Philippines (for rebellion)

. . . .

THE GULF WAR

. . . .

1. Iraq invaded Kuwait; 2. Kuwaiti oilfields; 3. Saddam Hussein; 4. France;
5. Iraq; 6. Soviet missiles used by Iraq; 7. US antimissile missiles;
8. Desert Storm; 9. US aircraft carriers; 10. A 1940s US Navy battleship used
in the war; 11. Iran; 12. George Bush Sr.

. . . .

THE 1980s

. . . .

1. Libya; 2. Mozambique; 3. Rajiv Gandhi, in 1984;
4. The price of oil; 5. Mel Gibson; 6. President Zia of Pakistan;
7. Toni Morrison; 8. Tunisia; 9. Nobel Peace prize; 10. Donald Duck;
11. Angola; 12. The pope

. . . .

THEY DIED IN THE 1990s

. . . .

1. Robert Bolt; 2. Peter Cook; 3. Rose Kennedy; 4. Jean Muir; 5. Ginger Rogers;
6. Jacqueline Bouvier Kennedy Onassis; 7. Kurt Cobain;
8. Lana Turner; 9. J Presper Eckert; 10. Maxene, of the Andrews Sisters;
11. Wilma Rudolph; 12. Pancho Gonzales

. . . .

ANSWERS
MODERN TIMES

· ·

POT LUCK 1980s

· ·

1. The America's Cup; 2. The wreck of the *Titanic*; 3. Ingrid Bergman;
4. Chernobyl; 5. Columbia; 6. Ronald Reagan; 7. He'd just escaped being
assassinated, but was wounded; 8. Zimbabwe; 9. Argentina; 10. Canada;
11. Lebanon; 12. Mulroney

· ·

1960s PEOPLE

· ·

1. A Mafia boss; 2. Chess; 3. Georges Pompidou; 4. New York;
5. James Meredith; 6. Jamaica; 7. The Central Intelligence Agency (CIA);
8. Presidential hopefuls Kennedy and Nixon; 9. The UN, as Secretary-General;
10. The Rolling Stones; 11. Sidney Poitier; 12. Johnny Carson
(*Tonight* show on NBC)

· ·

MORE 1960s STUFF

· ·

1. 1962; 2. Soviet Union (d 1984); 3. The new US strategic bomber;
4. Joseph Heller; 5. Robert F. Kennedy in 1968; 6. Czechoslovakia; 7. Vietnam;
8. Cuba; 9. Prague, Czechoslovakia (a student, Palach set fire to himself in
protest against the 1968 Russian invasion); 10. Lee Harvey Oswald;
11. Palestine Liberation Organization (1964); 12. Count Basie

· ·

MORE 1980s

· ·

1. They were dolls; 2. Photography; 3. His home state of Minnesota;
4. US ambassador to the UN; 5. Tom Watson; 6. Stalin's daughter Svetlana
Alliluyeva, who returned to the USSR; 7. Andy Warhol;
8. Soccer; 9. Richard Burton; 10. Literature;
11. The White House /US president; 12. Rupert Murdoch

· ·

ANSWERS
MODERN TIMES

· ·

1960

· ·

1. The Soviet Union; 2. The Kariba Dam; 3. Massachusetts;
4. The world's longest ocean liner; 5. *Psycho*; 6. Elvis Presley;
7. The spy plane was shot down by Soviet air defenses;
8. The Everly Brothers; 9. Cassius Clay, later Muhammad Ali;
10. South Africa; 11. Hollywood star Clark Gable, died November 16;
12. Soviet leader Nikita Khrushchev

· ·

LEADERS IN 1999... OF WHERE?

· ·

1. Czech Republic ; 2. France; 3. Sri Lanka; 4. Grenada; 5. Holland; 6. South
Korea; 7. Iraq; 8. India; 9. Ireland; 10. Japan; 11. Malawi; 12. Canada

· ·

1990s EVENTS

· ·

1. Commonwealth of Independent States (a post-Soviet Union grouping of
neighboring states); 2. Russia, Ukraine, and Belarus; 3. Russia;
4. Boris Yeltsin; 5. France; 6. Liberia; 7. Saudi Arabia; 8. Italy; 9. Weapons, he
led the UN weapons inspectors; 10. Thailand; 11. Chris Patten; 12. 1997

· ·

MORE FROM THE 1990s

· ·

1. Uganda; 2. Drugs; 3. Portugal; 4. Lesotho's King Moshoeshoe; 5. Mexico;
6. Afghanistan; 7. 1993; 8. Somalia; 9. Haiti; 10. Algeria; 11. Angola;
12. Germany

· ·

ANSWERS
MODER N TIMES

....

THE 1970s

....

1. Nigeria; 2. Amnesty International; 3. Turkey; 4. Spanish Sahara;
5. Marianne Moore; 6. Henry Kissinger; 7. China; 8. 1973; 9. Ghana;
10. The Boeing 747; 11. Cambridge; 12. A 1970 revue on the theme of sex in which some scenes contained nudity.

....

1970s NEWSMAKERS

....

1. Watergate; 2. General Franco; 3. Soviet ice skater who defected to the West in 1979; 4. Soviet foreign minister; 5. In Jordan; 6. Three airliners were hijacked by Palestinian terrorists; 7. Long-time director of the FBI;
8. The Russian answer to Concorde, a supersonic airliner;
9. Afghanistan; 10. Britain's Elizabeth II; 11. Andrew Lloyd Webber and Tim Rice; 12. Pakistan

....

MORE FROM THE 1970s

....

1. The Sinai desert, between Egypt and Israel; 2. Wounded Knee;
3. *Till Death Us Do Part*; 4. Golda Meir; 5. Gerald Ford; 6. Werner von Braun;
7. By being stabbed with a poisoned umbrella tip (he was a Bulgarian defector); 8. President Sadat of Egypt and Prime Minister Begin of Israel;
9. Afghanistan; 10. George McGovern; 11. Greece, after the ending of military rule; 12. Maria Callas

....

PRESIDENT REAGAN

....

1. 1980; 2. Republican; 3. Jimmy Carter; 4. "Dutch"; 5. "Where's the rest of me?" from the film *King's Row* (1942) in which he played an amputee;
6. Nancy (Davis); 7. California; 8. George Bush (father of George W. Bush);
9. Grenada; 10. Ceremonial trumpeters; 11. 1985; 12. Walter Mondale

....

ANSWERS
MODERN TIMES

. . . .

1980s CELEBRITIES LAST NAMES

. . . .

1. Gandhi; 2. O'Connor; 3. Retton; 4. Graham; 5. Sakharov; 6. Pinochet;
7. Gibson; 8. Haig; 9. Karajan; 10. Jackson; 11. Ueberroth; 12. Irons

MORE 1980s PEOPLE

. . . .

1. The Roman Catholic Church; 2. *Phantom of the Opera*; 3. Truman Capote;
4. Samora Machel; 5. Colonel Qaddafi; 6. Davis; 7. Poland; 8. Sudan;
9. North Korea; 10. Mario Cuomo; 11. Mitterand; 12. Michael Jackson

1980s AND 1990s TRIVIA

. . . .

1. Audrey Sakharov; 2. The Iran-Contra arms sales controversy;
3. Dr Seuss, author of *The Cat In The Hat* books; 4. Secretary-general of the
United Nations; 5. The Philippines, a volcano that erupted 1991;
6. Solo mountain climbs; 7. Marvin Gaye; 8. His father shot him;
9. An Iranian jetliner; 10. France; 11. Toys; 12. Belgium

MAKERS AND SHAKERS

. . . .

1. Algeria; 2. Egypt; 3. Clothes; 4. Kurt Cobain;
5. John F. Kennedy, at his inauguration; 6. The top hat; 7. India;
8. General Chiang Kai-shek; 9. The track, Algerian record-breaking runner;
10. The US presidency, but he never made it;
11. Wilt Chamberlain, US basketball star; 12. Mick Jagger

ANSWERS
ADVENTURE & EXPLORATION

121 PIRATES

1. Pirates working for a government; 2. Black Bart; 3. The Jolly Roger;
4. *Treasure Island* by Robert Louis Stevenson; 5. Captain William Kidd;
6. By being pregnant; 7. The Mediterranean; 8. Madagascar; 9. Edward Teach,
known as Blackbeard; 10. Sir Henry Morgan; 11. Jean Lafitte;
12. Somalia

122 EXPLORING AFRICA

1. The Niger; 2. The source of the Blue Nile; 3. John Hanning Speke; 4. Lake
Victoria; 5. David Livingstone; 6. The Zambezi; 7. The *New York Herald*; 8. To
find Livingstone, who had not been heard of for years; 9. Lake Tanganyika;
10. The Congo (Zaire); 11. Speke and Grant—they were traveling north along
the Nile, Baker was coming south from Cairo; 12. The French

123 EXPLORERS

1. The Pacific; 2. The *Santa Maria*; 3. Three; 4. Portuguese;
5. Brazil; 6. Columbus; 7. Samuel de Champlain; 8. The Pacific Ocean—the
first European to do so; 9. The first circumnavigation of the globe;
10. Navigation, in particular to determine latitude; 11. None (as far as it
is know), he sponsored many explorations; 12. Africa

124 THE NEW WORLD

1. Supposedly Amerigo Vespucci; 2. Florida; 3. Gold; 4. What is now the
southern United States; 5. Mississippi River—they were the first Europeans
to reach it; 6. In Mexico; 7. Francisco Vasquez de Coronado; 8. The Northwest
passage; 9. The east coast of North America; 10. Sir Walter Raleigh;
11. English explorer John Davis; 12. Beaver—for its fur

ANSWERS
ADVENTURE & EXPLORATION

. . . .

WHERE DID THEY EXPLORE?

. . . .

1. Australia; 2. Australia and Tasmania; 3. North America; 4. Hudson Bay, Canada; 5. The Pacific Northwest and Rocky Mountains; 6. The strait between Siberian Russia and Alaska; 7. Eastern Africa and the Nile; 8. The Canadian Arctic; 9. The Pacific, Australia, and New Zealand; 10. The Arctic (though his claim to have flown over the North Pole is disputed by some); 11. The coast of Antarctica; 12. Antarctica—led the first overland crossing

. . . .

ANCIENT EXPLORERS

. . . .

1. The Egyptians; 2. The Maori; 3. The coast of west Africa; 4. The British Isles; 5. Egypt; 6. Mermaids were reputed to lure seamen to their deaths; 7. A Moroccan traveler; 8. From China to the Indian Ocean; 9. The Vikings; 10. Greenland; 11. Probably Newfoundland, Canada; 12. Viking explorer Leif Erikson (son of Eric the Red)

. . . .

EXPLORING BY SEA

. . . .

1. Portugal; 2. An early navigation instrument; 3. A more seaworthy ship, used by Portuguese explorers; 4. Madeira; 5. The Cape of Good Hope; 6. Vasco da Gama; 7. He was an Arab pilot, who knew the Indian Ocean; 8. Ferdinand Magellan; 9. Five; 10. Spain; 11. The Philippines; 12. One

. . . .

BRAVE SAILORS

. . . .

1. Amundsen; 2. The Northwest Passage; 3. Henry Hudson; 4. France; 5. William Bligh; 6. The Atlantic; 7. Irish saint, whom legend has it sailed to America; 8. Francis Drake; 9. The *Golden Hind* (originally the *Pelican*); 10. Antarctica; 11. Fridtjof Nansen (Norway), drifting to the most northerly point then reached; 12. Around the world—first solo circumnavigation

. . . .

ANSWERS
ADVENTURE & EXPLORATION

....

HIGH FLYERS

....

1. Clément Ader (France); 2. Atlantic; 3. November 22 1977;
4. The parachute (1919 and 1922 respectively); 5. A flying machine with
flapping wings; 6. The Jumbo jet; 7. The first African-American pilot;
8. Jacqueline Cochrane (1953); 9. Glenn Curtiss; 10. First American woman
into space; 11. Charles Lindbergh; 12. 1927

....

FLYING FEATS

....

1. Byrd (1926, 1929); 2. North Carolina; 3. 1783; 4. J.F. Pilâtre de Rozier and
Marquis d'Arlandes (France); 5. Ruth Nichols; 6. First woman to fly solo
around the world (1964); 7. The V-2 rocket; 8. The Pacific; 9. Around the world
(first to do so solo); 10. Charles Yeager; 11. A helicopter;
12. First balloon crossing of the Atlantic Ocean

....

AMELIA EARHART

....

1. She became the first woman to fly the Atlantic solo; 2. The Ninety-
Nines, for women pilots; 3. Harbor Grace, Newfoundland; 4. In a field
near Londonderry, Northern Ireland; 5. A Lockheed Vega; 6. Two, Charles
Lindbergh and Bert Hinkler; 7. Soup and canned tomato juice;
8. To stop herself falling asleep; 9. 13½ hours; 10. From Hawaii to California;
11. 1937; 12. Fly around the world with co-pilot Fred Noonan

....

PIONEERS OF FLIGHT

....

1. Samuel Pierpoint Langley's; 2. *Flyer*; 3, Otto Lilienthal;
4. Paul le Cornu's twin-rotor helicopter; 5. Brazilian; 6. *14-bis*;
7. It flew tail-first; 8. Glenn Curtiss; 9. The world's first air passenger (1908);
10. Wilbur Wright (first American woman passenger in an airplane);
11. Octave Chanute; 12. Howard Hughes

....

ANSWERS
ADVENTURE & EXPLORATION

....

UP, UP AND AWAY

....

1. The Montgolfier brothers, June 4, 1783; 2. A sheep, a duck, and a rooster (1783);
3. François Pilâtre de Rozier; 4. October 15, 1783; 5. The balloon was tethered
by a rope; 6. Two criminals; 7. May 20, 1784 in Paris, four ladies ascended;
8. A hand-cranked propeller; 9. No; 10. De Rozier and Jules Romain died when
their balloon caught fire, while attempting to fly the Channel in 1785;
11. Blanchard of France, on January 9, 1793; 12. Thaddeus S.C. Lowe

....

FAMOUS EXPLORERS

....

1. The St Lawrence; 2. Samuel de Champlain; 3. The Great Lakes;
4. Auguste Piccard; 5. Australia; 6. South America; 7. Robert Peary (to the
North Pole, 1909); 8. James Cook; 9. Henry Hudson; 10. Thor Heyerdahl;
11. *Kon-Tiki*; 12. Cape Town, South Africa, 1652

....

MORE FLYING FEATS

....

1. Mme la Baronne de Laroche (France), in 1910; 2. Lt T.E. Selfridge, US
Army, September 1908; 3. Orville Wright; 4. Made the first takeoff from a ship;
5. First American woman to fly solo in a plane, 1910; 6. Austria, 1910;
7. A consignment of silk, flown from Dayton to Columbus, Ohio;
8. First American woman to gain a pilot's license, 1911; 9. First woman to fly
the English Channel in a plane; 10. Richard E. Byrd and Floyd Bennett;
11. Flew the Atlantic, with stops to refuel; 12. Captain John Alcock and
Lt Arthur Whitten Brown, in a Vickers Vimy (14/15 June 1919)

....

AMERICAN PIONEER LIFE

....

1. The Appalachians; 2. Daniel Boone; 3. On rafts; 4. Corn bread, for long
journeys; 5. The Conestoga wagon; 6. A river barge; 7. Filling up the gaps
between logs in a log cabin with moss or mud; 8. A community getting
together to erect a home for a new family; 9. To cover windows, instead of
glass; 10. Corn (softened in lye or water); 11. Turkey; 12. Home-made cloth
used for clothing

....

ANSWERS
ADVENTURE & EXPLORATION

. . . .

INTO SPACE

. . . .

1. Robert H. Goddard; 2. They said rockets could not work in a vacuum;
3. German pioneer, later designed US rockets; 4. Wernher von Braun;
5. Soviet launch vehicle used for first astronauts in space; 6. Yuri Gagarin;
7. In a plane crash; 8. US astronaut John Glenn; 9. Three; 10. Valentina
Tereshkova, first female astronaut; 11. Vladimir Komarov, 1967, killed during
re-entry of Soyuz 1; 12. First EVA or spacewalk

. . . .

AMERICAN ASTRONAUTS

. . . .

1. Virgil Grissom, who made the second sub-orbital flight in 1961; 2. Gus;
3. The first US two-man spacecraft (1965); 4. Fire broke out in *Apollo 1*
during a ground test; 5. Edward White and Roger Chaffee; 6. James Lovell;
7. Around the Moon and back in *Apollo 8*; 8. Its Moon flight had to be aborted;
9. James Lovell; 10. Command pilot of the two-man *Gemini 8*;
11. Edwin "Buzz" Aldrin and Michael Collins; 12. Aldrin

. . . .

EXPLORING THE WEST

. . . .

1. Meriwether Lewis; 2. Mapmaking; 3. The Missouri; 4. A Shoshone Indian,
she acted as interpreter to the Lewis and Clark expedition; 5. A US Army
surveyor and explorer of the West; 6. Kit Carson; 7. California; 8. Texas;
9. The battle of San Jacinto; 10. California—Los Angeles; 11. South Dakota;
12. Pioneer trails to the West

. . . .

MORE ABOUT THE WEST

. . . .

1. Paintings of Native Americans; 2. Davy Crockett; 3. Johnny Appleseed;
4. He wandered through Ohio and Indiana, planting apple seeds and
saplings; 5. Animal skins for trade; 6. The Shawnee; 7. "Big Turtle";
8. Davy Crockett; 9. Great Salt Lake; 10. Yellowstone;
11. Wyoming; 12. The Bozeman Trail

. . . .

ANSWERS
ADVENTURE & EXPLORATION

. . . .

THE WILD WEST

. . . .

1. Jim Bowie (1796-1836); 2. Wild Bill Hickok and Buffalo Bill Cody;
3. Buffalo Bill's; 4. His several jobs included hunting buffalo; 5. Deadwood;
6. Wyatt Earp; 7. Tombstone, Arizona; 8. Billy the Kid—in between, he
became William H. Bonney; 9. Pat Garrett; 10. Jesse James; 11. Frank James;
12. Judge Roy Bean

JOURNEYS OF DISCOVERY

. . . .

1. Four; 2. Portugal; 3. Rio de la Plata (Plate) in Argentina; 4. Magellan;
5. The ocean seemed calm after the stormy passage around Cape Horn;
6. Francis Chichester; 7. Around the world single-handed; 8. To the Antarctic;
9. Ernest Shackleton; 10. The Northeast passage; 11. Captain James Cook;
12. Edward Bransfield, 1820

THE FIRST FLIERS

. . . .

1. Wilbur and Orville; 2. Dayton; 3. Rev. Milton Wright was a minister of
the United Brethren Church; 4. Their father gave them a toy rubberband
helicopter; 5. A cycle shop; 6. Otto Lilienthal; 7. Gliders; 8. Kill Devil
sandhills, Kitty Hawk, N. Carolina; 9. 1903; 10. Wilbur; 11. Five; 12. Europe

LINDBERGH'S ADVENTURE

. . . .

1. Fly the Atlantic Ocean alone; 2. 1902; 3. Barnstormer—a stunt pilot;
4. A mail pilot, flying between St Louis and Chicago; 5. $25,000 to the first
aviator to fly nonstop New York-Paris; 6. Ryan Aeronautical of San Diego;
7. *Spirit of St Louis*; 8. Flew from San Diego to New York City with one
overnight stop; 9. One; 10. He could see only through a periscope, there was a
fuel tank in front of him; 11. Le Bourget, near Paris; 12. 33 ½ hours

ANSWERS
WORLD HISTORY 2

20TH-CENTURY HEROES

1. Roald Amundsen; 2. Neil Armstrong; 3. Anne Frank; 4. Nelson Mandela;
5. Martin Luther King; 6. Roger Bannister; 7. Hillary and Tensing;
8. George C Marshall; 9. Mother Teresa; 10. Alexander Dubcek;
11. Solzhenitsyn; 12. General Charles De Gaulle

GREEKS

1. Alexander the Great; 2. Sparta; 3. Making up their minds; 4. Persia;
5. Alexander; 6. Plato; 7. Agamemnon; 8. Helen of Troy's; 9. By the trick of the
Wooden Horse; 10. Aphrodite; 11. Jason and the Argonauts;
12. The Golden Fleece

400-700

1. China 605-610; 2. The Prophet Mohammed; 3. Columba; 4. Pope;
5. Japan; 6. Patrick; 7. The Vandals; 8. King Arthur; 9. Alaric's; 10. Attila;
11. The Byzantine Empire; 12. Persia

AFRICA

1. Angola; 2. Cameroon; 3. Comoros; 4. Djibouti; 5. Ethiopia; 6. Gabon;
7. Gambia. 8. Côte d'Ivoire; 9. Lesotho; 10. Liberia; 11. Malawi; 12. Mali

ANSWERS
WORLD HISTORY 2

149 TUDOR ENGLAND

1. In childbirth; 2. Cousins; 3. The Duke of Alencon (a suitor);
4. A sherry-type wine; 5. Archbishop of Canterbury; 6. Elizabethan ales;
7. Christopher Marlowe; 8. Sir Richard Grenville; 9. A company of actors;
10. Anne Hathaway's; 11. Henry VIII; 12. William and Robert Cecil

150 NATIVE AMERICANS

1. The Cherokee; 2. The Sioux; 3. The Hunkpapa; 4. Red Cloud; 5. Colorado:
6. A wooden frame pulled by a dog; 7. Buffalo (bison); 8. Touching a living
enemy in battle; 9. Dried meat; 10. Geronimo; 11. A mystical movement
among Indians, whose founders included Wovoka of the Paiute;
12. Wearing special shirts gave immunity to bullets

151 AMERICA IN THE 19TH CENTURY

1. Monroe; 2. Missouri; 3. 1848; 4. President William Henry Harrison;
5. Andrew Jackson; 6. The citizenship of African-Americans; 7. 1869; 8. Steel;
9. 1877; 10. North Dakota, South Dakota, Montana, and Washington;
11. Grover Cleveland; 12. The total length of railroad track in the
United States

152 ROME AND ROMANS

1. Rome and Carthage; 2. Horatius; 3. The Etruscans, led by Lars Porsena;
4. A she-wolf; 5. Julius Caesar; 6. Julius Caesar; 7. They were writers;
8. He was a gladiator who fought with a net and trident; 9. Mark Antony, to
Cleopatra; 10. Brutus and Cassius; 11. A warm-air central heating system
installed in Roman houses; 12. Plebeians—the working poor, better off than
slaves, but with very little

WAY OUT WEST

1. A stagecoach line (San Francisco to St Louis); 2. Wells, Fargo and Company; 3. The first Pony Express rider; 4. The transcontinental railroad; 5. Union Pacific and Central Pacific; 6. Freight wagon drivers; 7. A paddle-wheel steamboat; 8. To clear the track; 9. A small pistol, often concealed; 10. A crackshot entertainer (1860-1926); 11. Buffalo Bill; 12. Wild Bill Hickok, shot during a card game in 1876

JULY 4

1. Congress adopted the Declaration of Independence, 1776; 2. Pathfinder; 3. The Erie Canal; 4. John Adams, Thomas Jefferson, James Monroe; 5. Calvin Coolidge; 6. Garibaldi; 7. The Statue of Liberty; 8. The Philippines; 9. General Sikorski; 10. Jack Dempsey; 11. Marie Curie; 12. Paris

IN WHICH CENTURY WAS...?

1. 19th; 2. 19th; 3. 18th; 4. 20th; 5. 17th; 6. 15th; 7. 8th; 8. 13th; 9. 11th; 10. 19th; 11. 18th; 12. 11th

US STATES

1. 1783; 2. France (1803); 3. The 49th Parallel; 4. Spain; 5. 1845; 6. 1846, with the acquisition of Oregon; 7. Mexico; 8. Arizona and Mexico; 9. Alaska; 10. Vermont; 11. Virginia; 12. Utah

ANSWERS
WORLD HISTORY 2

....

ANCIENT EGYPT

....

1. The Nile; 2. The fertile region around the Nile; 3. Pharaoh; 4. "Palace";
5. The Sun; 6. The cat goddess; 7. Hieroglyphics; 8. Egypt's only female ruler;
9. The first pyramid; 10. Internal organs (liver, lungs, stomach, intestines);
11. In a tomb—they were models of servants, to help in the afterlife;
12. Making mummies (it was a mixture of salts)

....

THE YEAR 1776

....

1. A steam boat; 2. New York; 3. From United Colonies to United States;
4. San Francisco; 5. The Phi Beta Kappa society; 6. John Adams; 7. German
mercenary troops sent to America by Britain; 8. Captain Cook; 9. Gibbon;
10. Benjamin Franklin; 11. Mozart; 12. The Marquis de Sade

....

NAVAL HISTORY

....

1. Drake; 2. The *Sovereign of the Seas* (1637); 3. John Paul Jones;
4. English and Dutch; 5. HMS *Serapis*; 6. USS *Constitution*; 7. Traditionally
so blood did not show; 8. The United States (1775); 9. British and French;
10. The French; 11. The *Turtle*; 12. HMS *Victory* at Trafalgar

....

THE AMERICAN WEST

....

1. Cattle; 2. A Native American medicine man; 3. A Native American conical
tent of skins stretched over poles; 4. A Native American dwelling made from
brushwood; 5. The wagon carrying food for cowboys during roundup;
6. Paul Bunyan; 7. 19 months (1860-61); 8. A cowboy's rope;
9. Original half-wild cattle; 10. Meat dried, pounded and mixed with fat to
preserve it; 11. A wagon; 12. Horses, mules or oxen

....

ANSWERS
WORLD HISTORY 2

. . . .

161
THE YEAR 1492

. . . .

1. Ferdinand and Isabella; 2. Granada; 3. It was taken by Ferdinand and
Isabella; 4. The Jews; 5. Rodrigo Borgia became Pope as Alexander VI;
6. Lorenzo de Medici; 7. A Tuscan painter; 8. Three; 9. Japan; 10. Africa;
11. Portugal; 12. + and − signs

. . . .

162
MIXED BAG

. . . .

1. Buffalo, NY; 2. Benito Mussolini's; 3. Tutankhamun's tomb;
4. Brazil; 5. Vulcan; 6. Charles II; 7. 14th; 8. Wiley Post; 9. Australia;
10. Kemal Atatürk; 11. Ming; 12. Pigeon post

. . . .

163
AROUND EUROPE

. . . .

1. Austria/Austro-Hungarian Empire; 2. Austro-Hungarian Empire;
3. Belgium; 4. Italy; 5. Spain; 6. Denmark; 7. Five; 8. Louis XIV;
9. France, to Germany; 10. Greece; 11. Hungary; 12. Hungary

. . . .

164
TAKE YOUR PICK

. . . .

1. Copper; 2. Motorists changed to driving on the right; 3. California;
4. Japan's wartime prime minister; 5. 1949; 6. The Incas; 7. 1990;
8. French revolutionaries in 1789; 9. Andrew Johnson; 10. Italy; 11. 1917;
12. The first atomic bomb

. . . .

ANSWERS
CULTURE & SOCIETY

. . . .

SPORTS HISTORY

1. The New York Yankees; 2. None—retired undefeated world's heavyweight champion; 3. Chicago Bears coach George Halas; 4. Jimmy Connors; 5. Boxer Jack Dempsey; 6. Ben Johnson of Canada; 7. Ping Pong; 8. Argentina; 9. The Open golf championship; 10. 1881; 11. The Olympic Marathon; 12. Exhausted, he was helped over the finishing line

FANTASY AND HORROR

1. Tarzan of the Apes; 2. Alfred Hitchcock; 3. Edgar Allan Poe; 4. Dracula; 5. Mr Hyde; 6. Robert Louis Stevenson; 7. Shakespeare; 8. Turned them to stone (if they saw her face directly); 9. *The Hunchback of Notre Dame*; 10. Victor Hugo; 11. Frankenstein's; 12. A giant alien amoeba

ARTS AND CRAFTS

1. Canterbury; 2. Robert Burns; 3. Jewelery and especially jeweled Easter eggs; 4. Traditional carpets; 5. Auguste Rodin; 6. 18th; 7. Herodotus; 8. *Robinson Crusoe* by Daniel Defoe; 9. Furniture; 10. Saxony, Germany; 11. Don Quixote; 12. Portrait painting

FIRST IN THEIR FIELD

1. 1909 (Louis Blériot); 2. Walt Disney; 3. Oakland Raiders; 4. 1981; 5. The Matterhorn, he made the first ascent; 6. The first black male player to win the Wimbledon singles, 1975; 7. Phil Hill; 8. Fanny Blankers-Koen; 9. Youngest world no. 1 women's tennis player, at 17 years 3 months; 10. First woman to swim the English Channel; 11. *Dr No*; 12. By parachute—first parachute descent from a balloon

ANSWERS

CULTURE & SOCIETY

....

SPORTS IN THE 1960s

....

1. Athletics, he won the 1960 Olympic Marathon; 2. Northern Dancer;
3. The ladies singles at Wimbledon; 4. Joe Louis; 5. England; 6. Jack Nicklaus;
7. Ben Hogan's; 8. The New York Jets, winner of the Super Bowl;
9. Pancho Gonzales (aged 41) and Charlie Pasarell; 10. Gonzales, after 112
games—the longest match at Wimbledon; 11. He was first to use a
fiberglass pole; 12. Tokyo, Japan

....

VILLAINS

....

1. Lester J. Gillis, Gangster/bank robber; 2. William C. Quantrill;
3. John Dillinger; 4. The Emperor Caligula; 5. Sam Bass; 6. Al Capone;
7. The Son of Sam; 8. Timothy McVeigh; 9. The Wild Bunch; 10. Dr Crippen;
11. The serial killings of the so-called Boston Strangler;
12. Carlos the Jackal

....

MIXED BAG

....

11. Peritonitis; 2. Wink; 3. Peter Pan; 4. Josephine Baker;
5. London; 6. Jean Harlow; 7. Lucille Ball; 8. *Pygmalion* by George Bernard
Shaw; 9. Achilles; 10. Movie director Roman Polanski; 11. Apple; 12. Pop Art

....

CRIME AND PUNISHMENT

....

1. 1963; 2. Philadelphia; 3. Piracy; 4. Jack the Ripper; 5. A manhunt in which
everyone joined; 6. The electric chair; 7. Zodiac Killer (he was never caught);
8. To be hanged, drawn, and quartered; 9. Sir Thomas More;
10. San Quentin; 11. Ronald Reagan; 12. The guillotine

....

ANSWERS
CULTURE & SOCIETY

. . . .

SPORT AND LEISURE

. . . .

1. The Cresta run (tobogganing); 2. Basketball; 3. Billiards; 4. Ten-pin bowling;
5. Johnny Weissmuller and Clarence "Buster" Crabbe; 6. 1930s; 7. Tennis;
8. Muhammad Ali; 9. Jim Thorpe; 10. Greta Garbo; 11. Man o'War, winner of
20 or 21 races, 1919-1920; 12. The Stanley Cup

ANCIENT FUN AND GAMES

. . . .

1. Wrestling; he was a champion in the Ancient Olympics; 2. They competed
naked; 3. A Roman gladiator; 4. He despatched wounded gladiators;
5. A long fighting pole, used in medieval bouts; 6. A wooden sword; 7. Archers;
8. Firing arrows at tethered (or stuffed) birds; 9. Knights; 10. Trying to pierce a
ring with a lance, from horseback; 11. Chariot races; 12. Long jumpers

SPORTS ASSORTMENT

. . . .

1. 1851; 2. Bicycles; 3. The Gordon Bennett Cup; 4. Baseball;
5. Baseball, and it drew up the first regular rules; 6. Sonia Henie;
7. The Romans—it was a ball game; 8. The Aztecs in Mexico; 9. Iditarod;
10. Chess; 11. Horse racing—both were top jockeys; 12. He swam the English
Channel—the first person to do so.

CRIME FICTION

. . . .

1. The 87th precinct; 2. *The Thin Man*; 3. Simon Templar, Leslie Charteris'
The Saint 4. Agatha Christie; 5. Ross Macdonald; 6. Emile Zola (in the
Dreyfus case, 1898); 7. Mike Hammer; 8. Henry Fielding was a London justice
of the peace (from 1748); 9. Oscar Wilde; 10. Reading Gaol (England);
11. Sherlock Homes; 12. Professor Moriarty

ANSWERS
CULTURE & SOCIETY

. . . .

BELIEFS AND IDEAS

. . . .

1. Thomas Hobbes; 2, German; 3. Sigmund Freud; 4. Italian; 5. They met at the Stoa Poikile or Painted Porch in Athens; 6. St Peter; 7. The Prophet Mohammed; 8. India; 9. Lao Tzu in China; 10. Judaism; 11. He was the first Sikh Guru or teacher; 12. India

. . . .

POTPOURRI

. . . .

1. Polish; 2. Eros; 3. Herman Melville; 4. 4. By drinking hemlock; 5. Italy—though it was not one country when they were around; 6. France; 7. King Arthur's Knights of the Round Table; 8. The sky goddess; 9. Cicero; 10. The Jacobins; 11. Confucius; 12. Jeremy Bentham

. . . .

WHICH JOHN?

. . . .

1. Johnny Cash; 2. John Wilkes Booth; 3. Johnny Depp; 4. John Updike; 5. John Cassavetes; 6. King John; 7. John Coltrane; 8. John Williams; 9. John Denver; 10. John Mills; 11. John Maynard Keynes; 12. John Dillinger

. . . .

FAMOUS NAMES

. . . .

1. Joe DiMaggio; 2. George Gipp, an a college football star, who died aged 25; 3. John McEnroe, tennis player (to an umpire); 4. Thomas Alva Edison; 5. Frank Zoeller; 6. The 1986 New York Giants; 7. Boxer Joe Frazier; 8. He set an outstanding world record in the long jump at the Mexico City Olympics; 9. Marilyn Monroe; 10. 1950s US tennis prodigy Maureen Connolly; 11. First African American singles champion at Wimbledon, 1957; 12. Runner Paavo Nurmi (5 medals at the 1924 Olympics)

. . . .

ANSWERS
CULTURE & SOCIETY

· ·

MYTH AND MISCELLANY

· ·

1. Icarus—the wax melted when he flew too close to the sun; 2. Four; 3. Seven;
4. 80 Days (in the book by Jules Verne); 5. Water lilies; 6. Walt Whitman;
7. Borodino; 8. The American Civil War; 9. It was a dressing room;
10. Poseidon; 11. Britain's—a tanner was 6 pennies, a bob 1 shilling;
12. 1984—in his novel of the same name

· ·

ARTS ASSORTMENT

· ·

1. Russian, by Tolstoy; 2. Scotland; 3. France; 4. Henrik Ibsen; 5. The Ballets
Russes, Paris; 6. Vincent Van Gogh; 7. The sinking of the *Titanic* in 1912;
8. John F. Kennedy; 9. Winston Churchill; 10. Skyscrapers in the United
States; 11. The Beat movement—"beatniks"; 12. Frank Lloyd Wright

· ·

CULTURE MATTERS

· ·

1. War photos; 2. They were mobiles—moving works of art; 3. Three;
4. Nijinsky; 5. Julius Caesar; 6. A French mime performer; 7. Barcelona,
Spain—he was a Spanish architect; 8. Arms; 9. *The Pied Piper of Hamelin*,
by Robert Browning; 10. *Blithe Spirit*; 11. Blondes; 12. On the guillotine in
A Tale of Two Cities

· ·

OLD-TIME COUNTRY CRAFTS

· ·

1. Growing crops and raising livestock; 2. Hunting wildfowl such as ducks;
3. Barrels and casks; 4. Rabbits; 5. Sorting wheat ears from chaff by tossing
them in the air; 6. Butter and cheese; 7. A tool for cutting and shaping
wood; 8. Drove livestock such as geese and pigs to market; 9. A trap set by
gamekeepers to catch vermin; 10. Raking up corn left over after reaping;
11. Making and mending wagons; 12. Freight-haulers—drivers of carts

· ·

ANSWERS

SCIENCE & LIFE

. . . .

SPACE FLIGHT

. . . .

1. A V-2/WAC two-stage rocket was the first to reach outer space (about 250ml, 400km); 2. October 4, 1957; 3. Sputnik, launched by the USSR (Russia); 4. France, 1965; 5. The first US satellite; 6. The Moon; 7. A US space probe, landed on the Moon; 8. Venus; 9. First soft-landing on Mars; 10. The Soviet Shuttle (1988), later abandoned; 11. A Soviet space station (1986); 12. Mars

EVERYDAY TECHNOLOGY

. . . .

1. Wood; 2. Boiled bones; 3. Raising water, for irrigation; 4. Archimedes; 5. The Near and Middle East; 6. A steam engine; 7. 1930s; 8. The first battery; 9. Plastics; 10. The elevator; 11. The Romans; 12. The 1500s

DAILY LIFE AND WORK

. . . .

1. The cotton gin; 2. Microscope; 3. Louis Pasteur; 4. By preserving it in jars; 5. Washing machines (1860, hand-turned); 6. King C. Gillette; 7. Toilets; 8. London, the Bank of England, 1694; 9. Brooches or pins; 10. Sending Christmas cards—by the 1880s post offices were asking people to "mail early"; 11. Stethoscope; 12. Nitrous oxide as an anesthetic, 1844

INVENTORS AND DISCOVERERS

. . . .

1. Lister; 2. Penicillin; 3. A steam-driven vehicle; 4. Germany; 5. The pneumatic tire; 6. Henry Ford: the 1908 Model T; 7. Semaphore; 8. Printing press, about 1455; 9. First cheap ballpoint pens; 10. Frozen food; 11. Rutherford; 12. Insects: he and W.N. Sullivan made the first aerosol insecticide

. . . .

ANSWERS
SCIENCE & LIFE

....

MACHINES MISCELLANY
....

1. Miners' safety lamp (1816); 2. A steam locomotive—Stephenson's Rocket; 3. A one-man submarine; 4. The rotary car engine; 5. The air, it was a cross between a plane and a helicopter; 6. An adding machine he'd designed; 7. An early computer; 8. The first hovercraft or air-cushion vehicle; 9. Marconi (in Morse code), by wireless telegraphy; 10. An early record-player; 11. The sewing machine; 12. The Sinclair C5

....

STEAM SHIPS
....

1. The world's first turbine-powered ship, it could do over 60mph; 2. William Symington; 3. An American inventor and engineer (1765-1815); 4. *The North River Steamboat of Clermont*, or simply *Clermont*; 5. The Hudson; 6. *Olympic* and *Britannic* (originally *Gigantic*); 7. The Atlantic—first sail/steam crossing; 8. Paddlewheels; 9. From Britain to India; 10. I.K. Brunel; 11. First steamer to cross the Atlantic under steam power alone; 12. Screw (as tug-of-war tests demonstrated)

....

FOOD
....

1. Breakfast cereals; 2. The first fizzy water (carbonated); 3. The milk carton (Tetra Pak); 4. The chocolate ice cream bar; 5. Coca-cola; 6. 1930s; 7. Italians; 8. Germany (originally "Hamburg steak"); 9. A slice of bread used as a plate in medieval times; 10. The first sandwich (he was the 4th Earl of Sandwich); 11. Ice cream cones, at the World's Fair; 12. Baked beans

....

AROUND THE HOUSE
....

1. Scotch tape was invented; 2. The typewriter; 3. He invented a mechanical carpet sweeper; 4. An early tape recorder; 5. The vacuum flask; 6. To put out candles; 7. The first friction matches; 8. The first vacuum cleaner; 9. 1920s (1924 "Celluwipes"); 10. The first electric shaver; 11. The Chinese; 12. The late 1800s

....

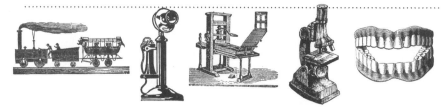

ANSWERS
SCIENCE & LIFE

....

FASHION

....

1. On the head, 1700s; 2. Britches, they were 18th-century suspenders;
3. Side whiskers; 4. A bra-like garment; 5. Jeans; 6. The bikini; 7. As fans;
8. General Ambrose Burnside (who prominently sported them);
9. The Chinese; 10. The 19th century—the word came from an Indian word
for "massage"; 11. A hooped petticoat (1500s);
12. Stockings were held up with tied garters

....

POT LUCK

....

1. A "helmet" hairdryer for home use; 2. The first supermarket shopping cart;
3. The Kodak camera; 4. 1980s; 5. Sugar; 6. The Egyptians; 7. Churches;
8. Furniture, especially 18th-century; 9. A medieval man's jacket;
10. The piano; 11. The first roller skates; 12. Monopoly

....

DRESSING UP

....

1. Ancient Greeks; 2. Minoan Crete; 3. Roman men; 4. Roman women;
5. The Ancient Britons (according to Julius Caesar); 6. On the head;
7. A long, straight coat; 8. Trousers, with wide bottoms; 9. Very pointed-toe
shoes, fashionable in the late 1950s-60s; 10. Around the neck;
11. A chain worn by a housekeeper, to carry the keys; 12. Hats

....

ODDITIES

....

1. The old name for sulfur; 2. Caligula; 3. The 19th century—James Ritter
(USA) made one in 1879; 4. He carried out the first heart transplant
operation, 1967; 5. Wash; 6. A rainwater spout;
7. With ether, this American doctor pioneered ether as an anesthetic;
8. Helen of Troy's; 9. UFOs first called "flying saucers"; it was a big year for
claimed sightings; 10. Hippocrates; 11. 1940s; 12. Volkswagen "Beetle"

....

ANSWERS
SCIENCE & LIFE

. . . .

INTO THE FUTURE

. . . .

1. Arthur C. Clarke; 2. Teletext; 3. The first industrial robots (1960s);
4. Samuel Morse; 5. Alexander Graham Bell; 6. A high-speed train (France);
7. Holography—making holograms; 8. The Mercury capsule *Liberty Bell*
(on splashdown); 9. 1970s; 10. The World Wide Web (Internet); 11. Far away
in space: quasi-stellar radio sources; 12. The Polaroid camera

. . . .

AVIATION HISTORY

. . . .

1. Howard Hughes; 2. A flying boat (the largest airplane ever);
3. First jet airliner; 4. Concorde; 5. The world's first airship; 6. Germany;
7. *Hindenburg*; 8. First jet plane to fly; 9. The Pacific, in a balloon;
10. Leonardo da Vinci; 11. Radar; 12. The Boeing 707

. . . .

POTPOURRI

. . . .

1. The Eddystone lighthouse—the model for future lighthouses;
2. Marine chronometers (clocks), to fix longitude; 3. 1700s; 4. Benjamin
Franklin; 5. Muslin; 6. The gas burner; 7. A servant (or a dog) that turned a
cooking spit; 8. Around 700-500 BC; 9. The contraceptive pill;
10. The aqualung; 11. The Egyptians; 12. Elastic (using rubber)

. . . .

ALL AT SEA

. . . .

1. The voyage of the *Marie Celeste* (the crew and passengers had vanished);
2. To protect the timber from burrowing sea-creatures; 3. A sailing ship of the
19th century; 4. Charles Darwin; 5. *Golden Hind*; 6. First US screw-driven
warship; 7. 19th; 8. *Rainbow Warrior*; 9. First nuclear-powered submarine;
10. It was the world's first "ironclad"; 11. The stern rudder;
12. The Confederate ironclad *Merrimack* (also called *Virginia*)

. . . .

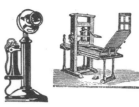